# Surviving as a Financial Consumer

By

Ken Pyzik

# Preface

Checking accounts, your paycheck, saving accounts, mortgages, credit cards, interest paid, interest earned, credit card interest, banking fees, car loans, home equity loans, stocks, bonds, investments, IRAs, 401Ks, and so on and so on and so on.

Throughout our lifetime, we are bombarded with a myriad of financial decisions that we have to make whether we want to or not. It is not unlikely that you will make a decision regarding your finances at least once a day, for the rest of your life. Yet most of us feel ill-prepared to make these decisions. We are not really taught about how to choose a good checking account in school. We rarely see a class on how to decide whether one mortgage loan is a better deal than another. I can't remember going to school to learn how to calculate the finance charge paid on a credit card. And, most of all, I don't seem to remember my parents sitting me down to talk about their finances.

So many of us are just in the dark when it comes to making some of these basic decisions that affect how well we may or may not do financially. Go over to a financial discussion at a party and suddenly you will see a bunch of people half-blitzed out of their minds with glazed over eyes as someone tries to explain some dazzling financial scheme. When was the last time you sat down with your kids and told them how you are able to calculate what your next mortgage payment is – and – NOT just what the statement tells you – but how they got those numbers?

It's amazing to me that so many people plow through their life, making decisions on financial matters without some basic tools available to help them make basic financial decisions. I find it appalling that our educational system finds little time to teach students such a basic task as balancing a checking account. I find it almost bordering on illegal the way mortgage bankers can sell an adjustable rate mortgage to a struggling family and sleep at night knowing that the people they just talked to could be heading for financial ruin.

Why is this stuff so complicated? Why, if someone tries to talk to you about this, do you shrivel up into a little ball and want to go away? Why do people seem to talk in circles and make no sense? Why, when it means so much to your future well-being, are you so afraid to talk about basic consumer financial stuff – stuff that is nothing more than simple mathematics? Why is this stuff such a big secret? These are some of the mysteries of life I don't think I will ever be able to answer. But one thing is certain – ignoring these things could affect your entire life.

I don't want to pretend to be some financial wizard that has all the answers to someone's financial well-being. People's finances are about as individualized as their political beliefs. Everyone has an opinion, and everyone's financial spending tolerance and spending habits are different. Some people like to live for the day, while others like to look out and plan 5-10 years down the road. No one book can tell you how you should live your life nor help you make every financial decision you will ever make. However, this book will give you basic information on how your lifestyle affects your financial decisions. It will present to you, in easy to understand terms, the basic workings behind how these things operate and why they are the way they are. It will show you how banks and credit card companies make money and how you, as a consumer, play an important part in their endeavors.

The purpose of this book is to teach you the basics behind consumer financial things that you encounter throughout your life. You will learn how and why things are structured the way they are so that when you are obligated to make a decision, you will choose the RIGHT decision that works for <u>you</u>. This book is about INFORMATION. This book is about teaching you things that your parents, your school, even your best friends, don't teach you when it comes to your finances - basic consumer money matters, and how these things affect your life.

# Table of Contents

# Chapter 1
# Money matters as a child

Your first lesson about consumer money matters probably happens when you are about 5 or 6 years old. You are driven to school, in your mom's beautiful debt-laden SUV, where you start to learn about dollars and cents and currency. Your parents, eager to help you learn what it is like to "work" or make money, explain that you cannot have every toy in the toy store and that "money" does not grow on trees. Ironically, even if money did grow on trees, it would not matter because your parents wouldn't know how to manage all that money!

Anyway, to get that nice shiny toy or that next candy bar from the candy store, you are told you have to start doing chores around the house -- take out the garbage, wash the dishes, feed and take care of the dog, change the cat litter box – you get the picture. Your parents are willing to give you money if you are willing to do the things that they don't want to do – or are too tired to do because they worked all day. You begin to place worth on chores – chore number one will get you one dollar, and chore number two might get you another dollar, and doing three or four chores might get you five dollars. Of course, the value of each chore is driven by how much effort you expend to complete the task. If it takes you an hour to do any particular chore, you might get a couple of dollars for it, whereas if it takes you several hours to do a chore, you might get five dollars for it.

As you begin to value the fact of "earning money" you probably, as most kids do, begin to think what you can spend it on. Forget about saving money – you are doing this for one reason – to spend, spend, spend! That nice bicycle seat or that great tasting hamburger at the local burger joint costs money – and you now have some money to spend. Your parents are relived that you are finally going to start buying your own stuff – even though they are still paying for it. It's a funny game parents play with their own minds. You are learning how to "handle money" – even though it's their money that they are giving you and they would be using it on you whether you managed it or not.

As a child, you begin to see through this game pretty quickly. If I do my chores, Mom and Dad will give me my allowance and I can buy stuff. If don't do my chores, I don't get the allowance to buy those nice toys or burgers, (even though Mom and Dad will still end up buying most of them sooner or later). It's a funny game played throughout many of the households of America – but it's a fairly decent tradition handed down for many generations to begin to teach kids about money. And, interestingly enough, it is a lesson that it taught so well, that most people do it for most of their life. If I work and make money, I can spend it on anything I want. If I don't work, I won't make money and I won't be able to spend it on what I want. Pretty simple – except for the fact that nowhere in this lesson is there any insight into – saving money, budgeting money, evaluating the pros and cons of spending vs. affordability, etc., etc.

Consider this -- have you and your children ever used the following logic:

"I want item X (something that is a little expensive). X costs 5 times my normal weekly allowance. If I work and save my allowance for 5 weeks, I will have enough to buy X. So that will be my plan".

Now – nowhere in this logic did you consider that within the next 5 weeks Mom or Dad might not have the money to pay the allowance. Or, nowhere was there a thought that something else you want may become more desirable and you might spend some of that 5 weeks' worth of money. Additionally, what if the chores are not completed well enough and you receive less than the full allowance, and thus, you didn't earn enough to really buy the item?

Using the same concept, parents can frequently be guilty of the same logic by buying the expensive item for you and stating that, after 5 weeks, the item will be paid off. This is a simplistic view of the "5 weeks same amount – item paid-off scenario". It fails to consider that "money flows in the future" are not always static. In other words, counting on and planning money or cash flows for the future is a tricky business that most people never learn to deal with. Changes happen and most people don't think to account for them. People have a tendency to not plan for possible contingencies and have a plan "B" just in case.

Unfortunately, this is exactly what we see in many young adults. They still use this simplistic view of financing and budgeting (since this is what they were taught as kids) and never get beyond the fact that future money flows are never exactly the same – they are always variable and should be managed.

Tragically, this may be the only true lesson that most parents give to their kids about consumerism, financial planning, and /or budgeting and finances. Typically, after the age of about 10 or 11, you are on your own when it comes to learning about personal finances.  So, if you are never taught anything else except this simple way of managing money and consumer behavior, how are you supposed to learn or act differently?  Hence – we have the first lesson about money matters that most people never learn:

1. "While it may appear that future money flows may be constant; they are never constant.  Changes will always occur and need to be considered BEFORE committing future money to anything."

Think about that for a second.  Future money – what is it really? Future money is money you *expect* or plan to get in the future. Children are very – very good at using their future money.  Some kids are so smart – they have their future money already spent one to two years out!  They have spent money which they have not even earned yet.   Does this sound similar to many 20-somethings or other people you know?

But there are several problems with future money that people never really learn or understand.  First, there is the issue of this thinking that future money is constant – it is not.  You can get close – but there will always be a wrinkle or a change that will alter the flow of this future money.

Second – and this is key – people think that future money is basically free.  In other words, when you are a kid and plan to spend 10 weeks allowance to pay for something now – whoever fronts you the money (usually a parent, grandparent or aunt/uncle) does not charge you any interest or service charge for using their money for *your* spending.   In the real world, or the adult world, people are not so generous.  If you are going to use my money to spend on something with the promise that you will pay me back – I am going to charge you to do that – since – you are spending my money RIGHT NOW. This is a very important concept you need to understand. For the privilege of spending future money – which is NOT a true certainty, you have to pay a fee, or interest. The reason you have to pay this fee is because money that is not future money is present money – here and now – earned. It is available to spend NOW. Future money is only possible money that may or may not come down the road. There is no guarantee that future money will come to you. If the future money does not come, you may be unable to repay the person who initially fronted you the money. Additionally, you should realize that the present money is not available for use by the person who fronted you the money, which isn't really fair to them to give it you to spend now for free.

Here, then, are three more very important lessons we rarely learn as children that we need to know when we become adults:

1.  Present money is ALWAYS worth more than future money. Money I have in my hands right now is worth more than a future promise of money. The reason: Money I have now is worth what it is worth RIGHT NOW – future money is basically worth less because it is NOT, and never can be, 100% guaranteed.

2.  For the privilege to spend somebody else's present money with a payment of your future money, it costs you interest or a fee or some other cost above and beyond your future money since, (see #1), future money is worth less than present money.

3.  While we never pay interest or fees when we are kids, in the real world no one is going to give you present money to spend today for the cost of just your future promise of

money in the future. (There are rare exceptions to this with cars being sold for 0% financing – but take my word for it, if you miss one payment – it is no longer free).

I think these lessons are the most basic that we can learn as a child. The next thing we learn as a child is the first time we get a job, usually around 15 or 16. That leads us to the next chapter.

# Chapter 2
# Paycheck Net Pay

For many of us, the true confusion of money matters really hits home the first time we take a real paying job for a company. The paper route job you had or babysitting jobs were pretty basic – you work so many hours, and the person in charge pays you a rate for each hour – say $5 an hour. So, you work 10 hours during the week, and you expect to get $50 – a simple $5 times 10 hours. So, this is pretty simple – and you are happy. Then comes the first time you get a paycheck from a job where you are working for a restaurant chain or retail store. Here, you are probably working more hours – say 20 hours if part-time, or 40 hours, if it is a full-time job. When they hired you, they told you that you would get $7 and hour, and you already have figured that you had worked 4 hours Monday night, 4 hours Thursday night, 4 hours on Friday night and 8 hours on Saturday – so that is 20 hours. You take your rate - $7, and the number of hours, 20, and you do the simple math – 7 x 20 = $140. You get excited waiting to see your first paycheck with that BIG $140 on it! You open the envelope to look at the check and you see $114.37?? What the?? What is this? You were supposed to get $140. Instead, you got this bogus amount. What is going on?? Suddenly, you have entered into the "real" world of financial matters.

*Ken Pyzik*

When you closely analyze the pay check, you see items on there that you have only seen for the first time. Something called "payroll deductions". You may see things like a taxes section. This section may include Federal Income Tax, Social Security (FICA) and Federal Medicare. You should see something that says W2 gross and net pay. As you get more important jobs, you may start paying for your medical and dental insurance. You could have optional life insurance. If you are working a union job, you may see a deduction for union dues. If you contribute to the United Way or other charitable organization, you may see a payroll deduction for that. If you decide to contribute to the company 401K program, you could see a deduction for that. If the company has a savings program that you have decided to take advantage of, there could be a deduction for that – and so on and so on and so on.

As you can see, the simplistic number of hours times rate per hour is a good way to "estimate" your pay – but it is rarely the pay you will receive. Additionally, many newcomers to the job market who are starting out will generally make the big mistake of budgeting their expenses based upon this simplistic view and quickly grow disappointed when they realize they have over budgeted for funds they simply will not "see".

To make this point a litter clearer, let's take a concrete example. Mary Ann, who just graduated high school and will be going to college in the fall, has accepted a job to work at the local retail store as a sales clerk selling young woman's clothing. Since she is just freshly out of high school, she will be willing and able to work 40 hours a week until she goes back to college in the fall. The Manager tells here she will be making $8 an hour. Additionally, as an incentive, if she can sell over $1000 worth of sales in the month, they will give her a $150 bonus – but she is not going to count on that. Also, if she works overtime, she will get a rate of

16

1.5 times her normal rate for the hours over 40. Mary Ann is very excited about this situation, and has started to "plan" what she will be doing with her earnings.

Here is the beginning of her plan: She will work from the beginning of June until the beginning of September – at least 40 hours a week. The manager has told her that she may average 4 hours per week overtime throughout the whole period of time. So – here is what she calculates:

40 x $8 = $320. Plus 4 x 1.5 x $8 = $48. So, the total is roughly $368 a week. The total time is 12 weeks. So, $368 x 12 weeks = $4,416. This is what she plans to earn. Mary Ann has her eyes set on some new clothes and accessories which are going to cost $500. She also wants to get a new phone which is $200 plus the monthly charge of $69. See also has promised to pay back her Mom and Dad $750 that she owes them. And finally, she wants to save $2,500 for college in the fall. So, $500 + $200 + $69+ $69+ $69 + $750 = $1,657. Add the $2,500 she wants to save, and she is at $4,157. Well, she sees that she plans to make $4,416 and her costs for the next three months will be $4,157 so she is in good shape – so far so good – right?

Think about this for a second. There are a number of flaws in the plan. Can you spot them? Let's go over them.
First and foremost – remember earlier in this chapter when we talked about payroll deductions. Mary Ann forgot to calculate, estimate, or at least guess at what those payroll deductions were going to be. Because of that, the $4,416 is over inflated. That is the absolute maximum she may earn. We already know it will be less because of the deductions. Secondly, she has calculated in overtime. The Manager has said she thinks she will average 4 hours of overtime a week. Well, what if they cut back and say no

overtime. Additionally, what if there is just nobody buying stuff and they decide to send Mary Ann home early on a few of the days. Already you can see that Mary Ann's earnings estimates are probably too high.

Therefore, we can come to two easy conclusions and lessons to be learned:

1. While it may appear that future earnings from your paycheck may be constant, they are rarely as predictable as you may like.
2. You always need to play it safe when trying to consider your future earnings from your paycheck BEFORE committing those future earnings to anything. Because they are future earnings (just like future money from the previous chapter), they are not 100% predictable until they are actually earned.

Now going back to Mary Ann's situation, we can see that she still needs to calculate in the payroll deductions. So, let's assume that she has minimal taxes taken, has no union dues, has no insurance since she is on her parent's insurance and she is not contributing to a company sponsored 401K or stock program. Let's make it as simple as possible. With that in mind, a good general rule for her would be to deduct about 17%. I use this figure since, basically, the FICA tax is around 6% and the Medicare tax is about 1.6% (these are general figures – not exact). The remainder would be her federal tax. If she was a higher wage earner, and if she was single, that 17% number would be higher and if she was married and had several children, you could use a smaller percentage. For the purposes of this book, we will use this easy figure. (To get a more detailed explanation of exactly how this is calculated, more information is provided in Chapter 6 – Basic Income Taxes). At this point we are just trying to get her close. Additionally, let's assume that she won't be getting any overtime or bonus money – and if she does – that is an extra bonus for her. Now the calculation looks like this:

40 x $8 = $320 – BEFORE payroll deductions – in this case – all taxes. The deductions will be 17% so $320 x.17 = $54.40. $320 – $54.40 = $265.60 per week. The total time is 12 weeks. So, $265.60 x 12 weeks = $3,187.20. Now we see that this is well short of the $4,157 she has planned to spend and save.

Now we have a more realistic earnings number. This is the true net pay, or "take-home pay", as we like to call it (the true amount of money she should expect to "take home").

While this may be a little on the conservative side, at least she is being cautious. Any overtime would increase that figure. Conversely, if she leaves early, takes a day off because she is sick, leaves early one day to go out with her boyfriend, or just does not work all 40 hours in one specific week – it could be less. Therefore, for purposes of helping her to plan – this is probably the best way to go.

Therefore, the takeaways from this chapter about paycheck net pay are:

1. Calculating your gross pay is easy. Calculating your net pay is much more complex and you need to take into consideration ALL payroll deductions, including – federal, state and local taxes, FICA and Medicare deductions, insurance and other benefit deductions (401K, saving plan), union dues (if applicable) and any contributions that you may have.

2. For purposes of considering your future earnings from your paycheck for spending purposes, always ONLY consider your net (take-home) pay not your gross pay. Considering your gross pay will lead to major disappointments since you will never take home that gross pay.

So, now that we have a better handle on paycheck net pay, let's move on to some other interesting topics.

# Chapter 3
# Balancing a Checking Account

Because the art of balancing a checking account is almost non-existent for anyone younger than 25, I almost decided to delete this chapter. But after thinking about the issues presented thus far, I thought it would be appropriate to at least talk about this subject so that people understand the basic mechanics and underlying principles that are at stake.

With the advent of online-banking and up-to-the-minute checkbook balancing information, it almost seems that the task of balancing a checking account should no longer be needed. But alas, regardless of how you do your banking, the same principles apply when it comes to determining your current cash situation (i.e., your checking account REAL balance). In fact, people get into trouble when they do not go through the process of doing a "balancing check" (the old task of balancing to your monthly statement) with their checking account – because they "forget" about outstanding checks, outstanding future auto-pay items they signed-up for, bank fees, etc. While the old-fashion "balancing your checkbook" task may be outdated – without understanding the principles behind it, you leave yourself open to some potential hefty overdraft fees and other bank "gotchas".

Having worked for a bank for several years, I can tell you – the bank loves that everyone can now do online banking. It is so simple for them to now say "just go and check your balance online". It is also easy for them now to say to you – "you should have known you were overdrawn – all you had to do was look online at your balance."

The fact of the matter is this – while online banking and checking account balance management may be much easier these days, many consumers still fall into a dangerous trap of committing their checking account balance to many things and then forgetting to account for them. Additionally, it is easy to not perform a balancing task (or as I called it – a balancing check) since the running balance is always available online.

For purposes of this book – I will discuss the old-fashioned way to balance a checkbook. Additionally, I will apply the same principles to today's online banking and show how the art of balancing your checking account balance still is important it today's online environment.

In the old days, you had a checking account, wrote checks, and kept a running balance in a checkbook so that you knew how much money you had in your account at any point in time. But as anyone who has a checking account can tell you, that balance that you see in your manual checkbook is NOT the same balance that the bank says is in your account at that specific point in time. It all has to do with the timing of when the checks "clear" your account (when the bank receives the actual check or transaction).

The best way to demonstrate this is to show an actual balancing statement -see below:

**Balance Your Account**

To keep track of all your transactions, you should balance your account every month.

1. List any deposits that do not appear on your statement on a separate sheet. Add then up and record the total (Outstanding Deposits total).

2. Check off in your checkbook register all checks, withdrawals (including Check Card and ATM) and automatic payments that appear on your statement. Withdrawals that are NOT checked off should be recorded on a separate sheet. Add then up and record this total (Outstanding Withdrawals total).

3. Enter the ending balance shown on this
statement here =====>                                   $ _____

4. Enter the Outstanding Deposits total here
=====>                                   $ _____

5. Total lines 3 and 4 here =====>           $ _____

6. Enter the Outstanding Withdrawals total here
=====>                                   $ _____

7. Subtract line 6 from line 5 and place
that number here =====>                                   $ _____

8. Enter in your register and subtract from your register balance any checks, withdrawals or other debits (including fees, if any) that appear on this statement but have not been recorded in your register.

9. Enter in your register and add to your register balance any deposits or credits (including interest if any) that appear in this statement but have not been recorded in your register.

10. The balance in the register should be the same as the balance shown in #7. If it does not match, review and check all figures used, and check the addition and subtraction in your register. If necessary, review and balance your statement from the previous month.

The statement here is from a major bank and it has been altered to fit here in the book.

Notice that items that have not "cleared" (items that are not reflected on the statement) are called "Outstanding Deposits" or "Outstanding Withdrawals." It is important to always keep track of all your transactions and to note any transactions on the statement that you either did not realize you had, or forgot, or just did not know were coming due (like a check fee for new checks, or an ATM fee from a bank where you withdrew money). As you can see, your checking account will essentially become this huge financial transaction ledger of your life!

Now let's look at the "new" checking account environment, or as they may say, checking in today's world. To give a more concrete example – let's say you open a checking account today and place $500 in there. This is the first checking account you have – and – up until recently, you have always paid cash for any bills or expenses. So now you have this checking account and you go to the local hamburger place to buy a double cheeseburger, fries and a drink. You don't have any cash, but that's OK since the bank where you opened the checking account gave you a nice shiny card that looks like a credit card (which it really is – but they have named it a debit card!).

That card gives you the ability to buy things without cash – by saying in effect, I have cash in my checking account and this card, when it is swiped, will let the merchant know whether there is enough money available in the account to cover the expense for the item you are about to purchase. So, you give the clerk the card – and she swipes it – and the card tells the register that, yes, there is enough money in the account to cover the cost (let's say it was $8.50) of the hamburger combo meal you want to purchase.

You take your meal and go on your merry way. So far so good. But let's analyze what essentially has happened. In the old days, let's assume you would not have had this card. So instead you would have had to pay cash (which you did not have) or, the store might allow you write a check. If you wrote the check, the merchant would be taking the chance that you did not have enough money in your account to "cover" the $8.50, and thus you would have written a "bad" check and the merchant would have been out the money. Additionally, if you have the money in your checking account to cover the expense, the merchant would have to deposit the check in their bank – their bank would then send the check to your bank – your bank would then deduct the money from your account – and finally the merchant would receive "their" money for your expense. This process is way too slow and complicated – and thus the debit card provides the merchant with the ability to know that you have the money in your account and they get their money right away.

There is a lot more involved in the process I just briefly described – but for purposes of this book – let's just say that the debit card is a blessing and a curse for your checking account. Now – back to our scenario. You purchase the item with your debit card, and the money is instantly deducted from your checking account. (Again – there is a little more involved here – but for our purposes, we will just say it gets deducted right away).

So now you have $500 less the $8.50 or, $491.50 in your account. You do this several times in the next month for let's say a total of $50 in expenses and thus you should have $450 left in your account at the end of the month. But there are other things you need to be aware of in order to "know" what the balance is in your checking account. Here are just a few examples of credits and debits that must be considered if you want to balance:

- If you have direct deposit of your payroll check, that amount must be added when the deposit go in;
- If you had some cash that you deposited;
- If you signed up for auto-pay for your phone bill or any other bill or items (e.g., the gym, Netflix, etc.);
- If you have a monthly fee associated with the checking account;
- Any additional purchases you made with your debit card;
- Any checks or other e-payments that you received from friends or relatives that got deposited;
- And, most importantly, you need to account for any checks that you wrote.

Thus, as mentioned previously, your checking account becomes a financial transaction ledger of your personal spending life. And, because it is, many people decide it is way too complicated to account for all these transactions, and so as long as they are close to what they think the balance is at any point in time – they are OK with that. And therein lies the first BIG - HUGE – bank "GOTCHA" for anyone who is new to consumer finances.

You see banks like that your balance is completely transparent. You can go online and see it anytime you want. But, as many young consumers and people new to checking accounts soon realize, if you are not good at keeping track of the transactions that affect your account, you may soon "overdraw" (i.e., commit too much money to pay for expenses for which you do not have enough money in the checking account to pay for). This process to the bank is, in effect, giving you an unsecured loan, and, thereby gives them free reign to charge you an overdraft fee (usually over $30), to charge interest on the money you overdrew (and that rate is quite high) and to continue to charge you fees for as long as you have that money overdrawn. This is one of the number one profit-making items for many banks! That is why they love to give you a checking account – because – most people forget about auto-pay items, or forget to deposit a check their parents gave them, or just over commit more than what they have. And when they do – the bank is more than happy to tell that you have done so and make themselves a profit!

That is why it is so important to "know" or least be able to get very close to knowing what the balance in your checking account is at any point in time – to AVOID overdrawing it and literally *give* the bank lots of your money for free for them to profit on.

So what is the best, recommended way to balance a checking account in today's modern banking world? Well, again, everyone is very individualized and has their own style – but the people who have never paid an overdraft fee probably do several of the following:

- Check the balance available on your account almost every day
- Jot down all "pre-authorized" pre-pay automatic debits and account for them every month ahead of time.
- Make sure to account for any fees, including checking account fees, ATM withdrawal fees, cash advances, and their fees, etc.

That transitions us nicely to our next chapter.

*Ken Pyzik*

# Chapter 4
# Basic Household Budgeting

I have to admit that this is probably the chapter that I most wanted to write. You see, I believe the thing that consumers hate to do most is probably to do a budget. Budgeting is a simple task, but it takes a lot of committed effort and patience to do correctly. Budgeting can be done many ways – and many budgeting books will probably do it differently than what I plan to present here in this chapter.

I have a pretty simple definition for budgeting: "Budgeting is making sure that you are spending LESS than what you are bringing in." Simple – to the point – factual – accurate and down to earth. It is really that basic. Let me demonstrate:

Are you spending LESS than what you are bringing in? If you can answer (or think you can answer) "Yes", HOW do you know (i.e., could you show me, if I asked)? Many people will answer yes to my initial question, but will be unable to show me how they know. If you can show me how you know, it will probably be because you are doing some form of budgeting. If you cannot, then you are one of the lucky people who has enough money to stumble along, unknowingly, living within your means.

If you are in the second group, you still may not be so lucky. Because, without proper budgeting (or knowledge of incoming income), you cannot ensure that future debts and outstanding expense will be covered by future income. Essentially that's what budgeting is - projecting future cash outflows (expenses) and assuring that future inflows (income, etc.) will pay for those expenses. When large companies do "projected" cash flows – they are essentially giving a peek into their future budget.

I like to think of budgeting in this way – Budgeting is a PROACTIVE approach (rather than a REACTIVE approach) to managing your money. Proactive means you are consciously performing a planned action. You are planning. Reactive means you are just letting things come at you and acting upon them as they come. You are just letting things happen and hoping for the best. Let's analyze this a little more closely.

Presented here is a table of six commons things a person should do to manage their money effectively:

| |
| --- |
| 1) List out your expenses |
| 2) Keep track of spending |
| 3) Plan purchases |
| 4) Make sure you get the most out of your money |
| 5) Set aside money for a rainy day |
| 6) Plan for financial freedom or independence |

This is a pretty good list of good habits you need to consider when trying to budget and manage your money. Let's look at the proactive ways these things are actually done vs. the reactive way many people really do them:

| **Proactive Action** | **Reactive Action** |
| --- | --- |
| 1. Listing out all your expenses for the month ahead of time | 1. Pay bills as they come |
| 2. Keeping track of things you spend on – even the little things | 2. Go to the ATM whenever you need cash for incidentals |
| 3. Planned purchases of <u>all</u> items | 3. Impulse buying |
| 4. Making sure you get the most out of your money or for your money by timing your purchases when things are on sale, etc. | 4. Spending on what you want when you want or need it because it is easier and convenient <u>(P.S. - YOU ALWAYS PAY FOR CONVENIENCE!)</u> |
| 5. Setting aside money for a rainy day – active saving | 5. If some money is left at the end of the month – put some aside for savings |
| 6. Experience the confidence of having financial freedom or independence | 6. Hope and pray for the best! |

As you can see, many people react to cash and money matters rather than proactively plan. The difference is significant. If you are doing more of the reactive items than the proactive items, you will quickly lose control of your finances and find yourself puzzled as to why you are always broke – or why you can't afford a new car or some other item when you need it.

Interestingly, many people can tell you these things, and, there are several books that will say these things. But, be real! We may agree that we should be more proactive in controlling the flow of our income and expenses. But what is a practical way to do this?

When I was faced with this problem many years ago, I created two spreadsheets. One spreadsheet was an "estimate" of expenditures and income (all cash outflows and inflows) for the entire year. I wanted to see where, as accurate as possible, I was going to receive and spend my income for everything for the entire year. I then duplicated that spreadsheet to track how well I did against my estimates. This second spreadsheet was an "actual" accounting of my expenditures and income. To demonstrate this, I have attached a sample spreadsheet (see next page).

20XX Family Budget

| | | Jan | Feb | Mar | Apr | May | Jun | Jul | Aug | Sep | Oct | Nov | Dec | Totals | % |
|---|---|---|---|---|---|---|---|---|---|---|---|---|---|---|---|
| | 1 | | | | | | | | | | | | | 0.00 | |
| | 2 | | | | | | | | | | | | | 0.00 | |
| VISA/CC | 3 | | | | | | | | | | | | | 0.00 | 0.00% |
| Other Debt payments | 4 | | | | | | | | | | | | | 0.00 | 0.00% |
| Savings | 5 | 5.00 | | | | | | | | | | | | 5.00 | 100.00% |
| | 6 | | | | | | | | | | | | | 0.00 | 0.00% |
| Internet Service | 7 | | | | | | | | | | | | | 0.00 | 0.00% |
| TV Service | 8 | | | | | | | | | | | | | 0.00 | 0.00% |
| Cell Phone service | 9 | | | | | | | | | | | | | 0.00 | 0.00% |
| Car/Truck Plates | 10 | | | | | | | | | | | | | 0.00 | 0.00% |
| Power (Electric) | 11 | | | | | | | | | | | | | 0.00 | 0.00% |
| | 12 | | | | | | | | | | | | | 0.00 | 0.00% |
| | 13 | | | | | | | | | | | | | 0.00 | 0.00% |
| | 14 | | | | | | | | | | | | | 0.00 | 0.00% |
| Life Ins | 15 | | | | | | | | | | | | | 0.00 | 0.00% |
| House Ins (Renters Ins) | 16 | | | | | | | | | | | | | 0.00 | 0.00% |
| | 17 | | | | | | | | | | | | | 0.00 | 0.00% |
| | 18 | | | | | | | | | | | | | 0.00 | 0.00% |
| Gas Bill | 19 | | | | | | | | | | | | | 0.00 | 0.00% |
| | 20 | | | | | | | | | | | | | 0.00 | 0.00% |
| | 21 | | | | | | | | | | | | | 0.00 | 0.00% |
| Car Payment | 22 | | | | | | | | | | | | | 0.00 | 0.00% |
| Car Ins | 23 | | | | | | | | | | | | | 0.00 | 0.00% |
| Oil/Gas/Maint for Car | 24 | | | | | | | | | | | | | 0.00 | 0.00% |
| | 25 | | | | | | | | | | | | | 0.00 | 0.00% |
| Health Ins (Med) | 26 | | | | | | | | | | | | | 0.00 | 0.00% |
| | 27 | | | | | | | | | | | | | 0.00 | 0.00% |
| | 28 | | | | | | | | | | | | | 0.00 | 0.00% |
| Church/Tithing | 29 | | | | | | | | | | | | | 0.00 | 0.00% |
| | 30 | | | | | | | | | | | | | 0.00 | 0.00% |
| | 31 | | | | | | | | | | | | | 0.00 | 0.00% |
| Entertainment/Vacation | | | | | | | | | | | | | | 0.00 | 0.00% |
| Total Budget Items | | 5.00 | 0.00 | 0.00 | 0.00 | 0.00 | 0.00 | 0.00 | 0.00 | 0.00 | 0.00 | 0.00 | 0.00 | 5.00 | 100.00% |
| | | | | | | | | | | | | | | 0.00 | |
| Quarterly/Monthly Assess | | | | | | | | | | | | | | 0.00 | 0.00% |
| REAL ESTATE Taxes | | | | | | | | | | | | | | 0.00 | 0.00% |
| Mortgage/Rent | | | | | | | | | | | | | | 0.00 | 0.00% |
| TOTAL CASH OUTFLOW | | 5.00 | 0.00 | 0.00 | 0.00 | 0.00 | 0.00 | 0.00 | 0.00 | 0.00 | 0.00 | 0.00 | 0.00 | 5.00 | 100.00% |
| **CASH INFLOWS** | | | | | | | | | | | | | | | |
| Interest | | | | | | | | | | | | | | 0.00 | |
| Pensions/Ret.Inc/other | | | | | | | | | | | | | | 0.00 | |
| Work Check 1 | | 100.00 | | | | | | | | | | | | 100.00 | |
| Work Check 2 | | | | | | | | | | | | | | 0.00 | |
| Deposits | | | | | | | | | | | | | | 0.00 | |
| TOTAL CASH INFLOW | | 100.00 | 0.00 | 0.00 | 0.00 | 0.00 | 0.00 | 0.00 | 0.00 | 0.00 | 0.00 | 0.00 | 0.00 | 100.00 | |
| NET CASH FLOW | | 95.00 | 0.00 | 0.00 | 0.00 | 0.00 | 0.00 | 0.00 | 0.00 | 0.00 | 0.00 | 0.00 | 0.00 | 95.00 | |
| | | | | | | | | | | | | | | | |
| Savings | | 105.00 | 105.00 | 105.00 | 105.00 | 105.00 | 105.00 | 105.00 | 105.00 | 105.00 | 105.00 | 105.00 | 105.00 | | |

If you place everything you know you have to spend on in the spreadsheet, you can make a total "financial spending plan" for the entire year. Clearly, there will be "unplanned" expenses. But that is the beauty of the plan. Mapping out all "known" expenses for the year provides you the following benefits:

- You know when major "one a year" or once every x month's expenses will be coming due. For example – car insurance (if you don't pay monthly), home owner's insurance (if it is not included in your monthly mortgage), license plates and vehicle registration fees, sewer fees (if they are annual) or any other periodic or annual fees;
- You can prepare for monthly expenses. For example, rent or mortgage, utilities, credit card bills (if you have them), health insurance premiums (if you don't pay through work), etc.;
- You have a knowledge of all incoming income; your paycheck, any monthly payments received, pensions or retirement checks (if you get them), etc.
- By totaling each row, you can actually see if you have more money coming in (income) than you have going out (spending). If you see a red number at the bottom – you are spending more than you are making! (BINGO – isn't that what we said the definition of budgeting really was?)

Even more exciting is this: remember that I told you that I originally had two of these spreadsheets. One was for all the income and expenses I *expected* (planned) to occur for the year – and one was for all the income and expenses that *actually* occurred. Now if you combine the two, you can give yourself a window into what you actually have spent compared to what you are anticipating to spend and bring in for the rest of the year.

While this takes a little effort to do and it takes away the budget number you had for months that have passed, it allows you to plan for what is ahead and see if you can (or cannot) afford something in the future. (I use shading or colors to delineate between the planned items and the actual things that have occurred). Here is what this looks like (an example of the combined actual/planned budget for the year, on the next page).

(Notice in this example the part that is shaded is what you plan or expect to spend and bring in. The White or unshaded area is what you have actually spent.

From the example you can see that this person has done a very good job of planning and the number at the end is a positive number. Thus, they will bring in more money than they have spent or committed to spend.) (Note that the utilities are the same for every month. I recommend this for most people as this is a great way to budget your costs.)

Until now, we have covered subjects dealing with personal finance and money matters for an individual. The next chapter will look at financial matters from an overall consumer standpoint.

Ken Pyzik

## 20XX Personal Budget

| | | Jan | Feb | Mar | Apr | May | Jun | Jul | Aug | Sep | Oct | Nov | Dec | Totals | % |
|---|---|---|---|---|---|---|---|---|---|---|---|---|---|---|---|
| | 1 | | | | | | | | | | | | | 0.00 | |
| | 2 | | | | | | | | | | | | | 0.00 | |
| VISA/CC | 3 | 50.00 | 50.00 | 50.00 | 50.00 | 50.00 | 50.00 | 50.00 | 50.00 | 50.00 | 50.00 | 50.00 | 50.00 | 600.00 | 2.35% |
| Other Debt payments | 4 | 175.00 | 175.00 | 175.00 | 175.00 | 175.00 | 175.00 | 175.00 | 175.00 | 175.00 | 175.00 | 175.00 | 175.00 | 2100.00 | 8.22% |
| Savings | 5 | 150.00 | 150.00 | 150.00 | 150.00 | 150.00 | 150.00 | 150.00 | 150.00 | 150.00 | 150.00 | 150.00 | 150.00 | 1800.00 | 7.04% |
| | 6 | | | | | | | | | | | | | 0.00 | 0.00% |
| Internet/TV Service | 7 | 101.75 | 101.75 | 101.75 | 101.75 | 101.75 | 101.75 | 101.75 | 101.75 | 101.75 | 101.75 | 101.75 | 101.75 | 1221.00 | 4.78% |
| | 8 | | | | | | | | | | | | | 0.00 | 0.00% |
| Cell Phone service | 9 | 52.34 | 52.34 | 52.34 | 52.34 | 52.34 | 52.34 | 52.34 | 52.34 | 52.34 | 52.34 | 52.34 | 52.34 | 628.08 | 2.46% |
| Car/Truck Plates | 10 | | | | | 78.00 | | | | | | | | 78.00 | 0.31% |
| Power (Electric) | 11 | 45.00 | 45.00 | 45.00 | 45.00 | 45.00 | 45.00 | 45.00 | 45.00 | 45.00 | 45.00 | 45.00 | 45.00 | 540.00 | 2.11% |
| | 12 | | | | | | | | | | | | | 0.00 | 0.00% |
| | 13 | | | | | | | | | | | | | 0.00 | 0.00% |
| | 14 | | | | | | | | | | | | | 0.00 | 0.00% |
| Life Ins | 15 | | | | | | 278.00 | | | | | | | 278.00 | 1.09% |
| Condo Ins. | 16 | | 335.00 | | | | | | | | | | | 335.00 | 1.31% |
| | 17 | | | | | | | | | | | | | 0.00 | 0.00% |
| | 18 | | | | | | | | | | | | | 0.00 | 0.00% |
| Gas Bill | 19 | 20.00 | 20.00 | 20.00 | 20.00 | 20.00 | 20.00 | 20.00 | 20.00 | 20.00 | 20.00 | 20.00 | 20.00 | 240.00 | 0.94% |
| | 20 | | | | | | | | | | | | | 0.00 | 0.00% |
| | 21 | | | | | | | | | | | | | 0.00 | 0.00% |
| Car Payment | 22 | 250.00 | 250.00 | 250.00 | 250.00 | 250.00 | 250.00 | 250.00 | 250.00 | 250.00 | 250.00 | 250.00 | 250.00 | 3000.00 | 11.74% |
| Car Ins | 23 | 75.00 | 75.00 | 75.00 | 75.00 | 75.00 | 75.00 | 75.00 | 75.00 | 75.00 | 75.00 | 75.00 | 75.00 | 900.00 | 3.52% |
| Oil/Gas/Maint for Car | 24 | 72.73 | 65.23 | 60.00 | 78.50 | 89.53 | 75.00 | 75.00 | 75.00 | 75.00 | 75.00 | 75.00 | 75.00 | 890.99 | 3.49% |
| | 25 | | | | | | | | | | | | | 0.00 | 0.00% |
| Unexpected Expense | 26 | | 212.30 | | 73.00 | | | | | | | | | 285.30 | 1.12% |
| | 27 | | | | | | | | | | | | | 0.00 | 0.00% |
| | 28 | | | | | | | | | | | | | 0.00 | 0.00% |
| | 29 | | | | | | | | | | | | | 0.00 | 0.00% |
| | 30 | | | | | | | | | | | | | 0.00 | 0.00% |
| Misc Cash Expense | 31 | 120.00 | 120.00 | 60.00 | 80.00 | 80.00 | 80.00 | 80.00 | 80.00 | 80.00 | 80.00 | 80.00 | 80.00 | 1020.00 | 3.99% |
| Entertainment/Vacation | | | | | | | | | | | | | | 0.00 | 0.00% |
| Total Budget Items | | 1111.82 | 1651.62 | 1039.09 | 1150.59 | 1166.62 | 1352.09 | 1074.09 | 1074.09 | 1074.09 | 1074.09 | 1074.09 | 1074.09 | 13916.37 | 54.45% |
| | | | | | | | | | | | | | | 0.00 | |
| Quarterly/Monthly Assess | | 45.00 | 45.00 | 45.00 | 45.00 | 45.00 | 45.00 | 45.00 | 45.00 | 45.00 | 45.00 | 45.00 | 45.00 | 540.00 | 2.11% |
| REAL ESTATE Taxes | | 375.87 | | | 375.87 | | | 375.87 | | | 375.87 | | | 1503.48 | 5.88% |
| Mortgage/Rent | | 800.00 | 800.00 | 800.00 | 800.00 | 800.00 | 800.00 | 800.00 | 800.00 | 800.00 | 800.00 | 800.00 | 800.00 | 9600.00 | 37.56% |
| TOTAL CASH OUTFLOW | | 2332.69 | 2496.62 | 1884.09 | 2371.46 | 2011.62 | 2197.09 | 2294.96 | 1919.09 | 1919.09 | 2294.96 | 1919.09 | 1919.09 | 25559.85 | 100.00% |
| CASH INFLOWS | | | | | | | | | | | | | | | |
| Interest | | | | | | | | | | | | | | 0.00 | |
| Pensions/Ret.Inc/other | | | | | | | | | | | | | | 0.00 | |
| Work Check 1 | | 1328.73 | 1328.73 | 1328.73 | 1328.73 | 1328.73 | 1328.73 | 1328.73 | 1328.73 | 1328.73 | 1328.73 | 1328.73 | 1328.73 | 15944.76 | |
| Work Check 2 | | 1328.73 | 1328.73 | 1328.73 | 1328.73 | 1328.73 | 1328.73 | 1328.73 | 1328.73 | 1328.73 | 1328.73 | 1328.73 | 1328.73 | 15944.76 | |
| Deposits | | | | | | | | | | | | | | 0.00 | |
| TOTAL CASH INFLOW | | 2657.46 | 2657.46 | 2657.46 | 2657.46 | 2657.46 | 2657.46 | 2657.46 | 2657.46 | 2657.46 | 2657.46 | 2657.46 | 2657.46 | 31889.52 | |
| NET CASH FLOW | | 324.77 | 160.84 | 773.37 | 286.00 | 645.84 | 460.37 | 362.50 | 738.37 | 738.37 | 362.50 | 738.37 | 738.37 | 6329.67 | |

# Chapter 5
# Grocery Store Value Comparisons (Unit Pricing)

The next most important thing, from a consumer's standpoint, that affects your pocketbook, and an item where you have some control, would be at the supermarket. While there are mountains of books that talk about couponing, buying in bulk, and other schemes to help an everyday consumer save on the grocery budget, a more basic concept to explore (and expose to consumers) is value comparison - price per serving/ per ounce/ or per item – or what is known as unit pricing.

Having worked for a consumer products companies, realizing how they make money was a valuable lesson for me. Although the consumer products industry is important and reputable, consumers need to know some of the tricks of the trade when it comes to purchasing consumer products – particularly groceries.

For most grocery shoppers, a trip to the grocery store begins with making a list of things they need, like fresh fruits, vegetables, packaged goods, meats, dairy products, bread, drinks, etc. (Some people, do not make a list – which is alarming since it means they don't care about value comparisons). Typically, consumers will have brands they are fond of, and, will purchase those items that they know and have had a good experience with. Some consumers may, and I say may since many do not, browse the sales flyer to see if something is on sale (e.g., a particular box of cereal). They then will decide to purchase the sale item instead of a substitute product (a box of oatmeal) or instead of their normal product (cereal brand X rather than cereal brand Y). That is all well and good – and the consumer is happy and they believe they have saved money, and that usually is the case.

However, there are several conscious things that you should do besides just buying things that are on sale. Frequently, buying sales items may not be the best value. How many times have you gone to the store saying to yourself -- "I think I'll spend about $50 today -- I saw several items on sale that I need or want in addition to two or three other items, and if I buy the items on sale with the other items, it should cost about $50?" You purchased the items, and found that after you bought all the stuff you planned to buy you actually spent $65 or $70. Sound familiar? The reason why is -- just because an item is on sale does not necessarily mean that it is less expensive to buy from the item that you would normally buy.

Let's consider this issue from a "value comparison" or a unit pricing perspective. Coffee is an excellent example of value comparison, because, a few years ago, before Starbucks came on the scene, economists found that consumers were very "elastic" in their demand for coffee. (Elastic means that just a small change in the price would cause consumers to switch to a less expensive brand). Most coffees tasted the same so there was not that much difference between brand A or B.

Coffee used to come in one, two and three pound cans. Coffee was priced by the pound. Although brands were comparable – you paid a premium for nationally recognized brands. Store and generic brands were almost always a little less expensive. When raw coffee prices went up, the price for a pound of coffee went up and when raw coffee prices went down, you actually sometimes saw a decrease in coffee prices by the pound in the retail store. All was pretty consistent.

Interestingly, this worked well until consumer products companies began to realize that they weren't making much money on a pound of coffee. Increasing the price would mean losing market share since, you could buy a pound of coffee from a different company for the cheaper price. To sell more than their competitor, they could drop their price on a pound of coffee and more consumers would buy their brand. So, to change things up and muddy up the market, the consumer products companies began to tinker with the packaging and sizes. They dropped the price on a "pound" of coffee and you *thought* you were getting a better deal – until you looked at the coffee can and realized that instead of 1lb of coffee (16 oz.) you actually were getting 14.5 oz. So, the price per ounce (or what is called the *unit price* – the price per unit) was actually costing you more.

Today it is difficult to find a 1lb, 2lb or 3lb can of coffee. What used to be a 1lb can is now 12 or 14 oz. The two pound cans are 28 or some odd number of ounces and the three pound cans are somewhere in the 30-35 oz. range (significantly different than what they used to be).

Did consumer products companies do this to thoroughly confuse consumers or to trick them? Well, not really. It was a way to make more money on a commodity product. Most consumers were used to going to the store to buy their normal 1lb or 2lb or 3lb can of coffee and, as long as the price was pretty much the same as it was before, and not too much more or less than the competitor's price, they were good. But what has happened today is that the price comparison is no longer an "apples to apples" comparison. If company A prices their 30.5 oz. can at $7 whereas company B prices their 31.4 oz. can at $7.50, which is the better deal? If you don't care about the brand and in your eyes the quality is the same – which is really the better deal for you? Where are you getting the best value? To make matters worse, some manufactures stopped placing coffee in cans and started to place in bags. Or they changed the packaging and placed it a paper brick type packaging. Trying to compare one brand to the other has become very confusing.

Happily, there still is a way to do a price comparison. Several years ago, consumer protection agencies asked states to require grocery stores to post "Price per unit pricing". Some states do this, some do not. However, even if it is not required, many grocery stores will provide the unit pricing. If you go to a reputable grocery store today almost every product will have a price per unit pricing on it – yet most consumers don't use it.

So, if you go to the store to buy olive oil, you will find the "price per ounce" numbers next to the price. All of the brands will have it and you may notice that the price per ounce will vary widely and significantly. If you like brand A and it is 50 cents per ounce, is it really worth it if the store brand is only 25 cents per ounce. Is buying brand A worth DOUBLE the unit price??

Now think about all the things you have bought at the grocery store. Cookies, crackers, a can of stew, coffee, chips, and so on. Almost every grocery product, with the exception of milk (gallon) and eggs (a dozen), has probably experienced a change in the packaging that has resulted in a new "price per unit" pricing.

So, as a value conscience consumer who desires to get the most value for their money, what is the best thing to do? It is best to at least analyze and be aware of the price per unit pricing. In the olive oil example, I noticed that I was able to get a good size bottle of olive oil for HALF the price of a different brand by using the price per ounce instead of the price of the actual product only. Let's use another example to emphasize this point. Sugar is a pretty simple commodity. There is probably not a big difference in brand A and brand B of sugar (although the manufactures would like you to think so). Do you find one brand of sugar sweeter than another?

Sugar usually comes in a 5 lb. bag. Let's say you really don't want to buy that much and so you go to look for something a little smaller. There is a two and ¼ lb. bag for $1.99 and there is a one and ¾ lb. bag for 1.69? Which is the better value?? Can you figure it out?

That's correct – use the price per unit pricing (which, should be provided in the grocery isle for you to see). You look for the price per oz. and find that the larger bag is 5 ½ cents per oz. (1.99 / 36) and the smaller bag is 6 cents per oz. (1.69 / 28). So, the larger bag is a better value. Since the difference is small, you may just want to spend the 1.69 instead of the 1.99 if you don't use that much sugar. But, had there been a significant difference, you now have the information you need to make an informed decision.

On the other hand, in the olive oil example the difference was more pronounced. When I looked at the price per oz., one was 50 cents per oz. and the other was 25 cents per oz. So, since I did not have preference in the taste of one over the other, I chose to get double my money's worth by selecting the one with the lower price per oz.

The moral to this chapter is that in order to get a true look at the price of a grocery product, you need to look at the unit price, the price per unit, to see if you are getting the "best" value for your dollar. This is not to say that you should purchase the least expensive item all the time – if you don't mind paying a little extra for a premium product - you should do that. At least you'll know whether the premium you are paying is really worth the additional cost. By using the price per unit - you will have a true value comparison and negate the consumer products companies trick to confuse you by shrinking product sizes but maintaining the same price.

If you are not good in math or calculating unit price, download a Google app for your Android phone for free called – "Unit Price Compare". Use it and I think you will be pleasantly surprised.

The second moral is to always be cognizant when packaging of an item changes. Almost always, the packaging change will result in either lesser of the product (smaller quantity) or a higher price for the same amount of product. Use the price per unit pricing to alert you to true price increases (not the price of the product). If you pay attention to this, you may actually save some money and/or get more value for your money the next time you go to the grocery store.

# Chapter 6
# Basic Income Taxes

After groceries, the next area of consumer finance where most people do not pay attention and/or really feel they have no control – but do – is income taxes. Most individual's first exposure to income taxes is when they get their first job with a real paycheck. Aside from knowing that the government always get a slice of your income (hence the name – income taxes), few people understand why, how much, and how they can control what is taken from their paycheck. This chapter will shed some light on this topic.

First – let's look at the why. This is a philosophical and political answer as opposed to a truly financial answer. Basically, in order for the government to function and provide services like roads, security and protection (i.e., a military), welfare services, funds for federal parks, etc., the government needs money. The only way they get that money is to tax. Placing a tax on personal property, fees for licensing, etc. are all government levies to fund the goods and services that a government feels it needs to provide its citizens. One can argue whether they spend the money wisely – but that is topic for a whole different book!

Another tax is a tax on your income. That's right – the government gets a slice of your hard earned pay. Now there are scholars who will argue whether this is legal or not – but again – without wading into a political quagmire – let's just say that the government has decided that they have the right to take a slice of your pay to help fund the products and services they need to provide for its citizens.

So, how much does the government get to take? Well, the amount they take has always changed from year to year which makes it difficult for most folks to plan how much will be taken so they can properly budget. It is not impossible to do – just difficult. But since it is a little hard or complicated, most folks just accept that the government is going to take some money, wait for their first paycheck, and then plan from there. Although this is better than not planning at all – it leaves a lot to on the table that you as a consumer could better control. Let's examine more closely how much the government will take from your paycheck for taxes and how you can control it.

First – how can you determine how much the government will take from your paycheck? (This is technically called Tax Withholding – the amount the government requires your employer to "withhold" from your paycheck every pay period). Calculating the tax "withholding" from your paycheck depends on a couple of things:

- How much you make for every pay period
- How often you get paid (i.e., your pay period – weekly, bi-weekly, twice a month, etc.)
- How many "exemptions" you are allowed and/or you have indicated that you plan to take. *(This is a key item I will discuss later).*

For simplicity, let's say you make $1,000 a week and you get paid every two weeks. So that would mean the pay period is bi-weekly and you get $2,000 every pay period. Now, again for purposes of showing this example, let's say you are single and have decided to take 1 exemption (again – *I will explain the significance of this item in much more detail later)*.

We will use the tables on the next few pages to calculate the withholding tax (**these tables are for 2015**. The tables change every year and are published by the IRS. Make sure to use the right tables for the year you want to estimate). Most companies have payroll programs that do this automatically – but it is important for you to know how the calculation is done.

First – there are three items we will calculate – The Social Security Tax, the Medicare Tax, and the Federal Income Tax (withholding). State Income tax rates are different for each state. I live in Nevada, where there is no state tax (good for me!), - but the calculation is simple once you know the rate.

The first table indicates that the Social Security tax rate is 6.2% for all earnings up to $118,500 annually in 2015. Since you make $1,000 a week ($52,000 a year) you fall in this range. The calculation is simple:  $2000 (earnings for the period) x .062 (the percentage is decimal terms) = **$124.**

Next, we use the first table again for the Medicare tax. The rate is 1.45% for ALL earnings. If you are fortunate enough to make over $200,000 a year, you would need to pay an additional .9% for the excess over $200,000. You are not one of the fortunate ones so your calculation is simple:  $2000 (earnings for the period) x .0145 (the percentage in decimals terms) = **$29**

Now let's do the federal income tax. This is a little more complicated. Here are the steps:
   1.  First, find your pay period (in our case it is biweekly)

2. Next, find what the gross pay is (in our case $2000)
3. Add up your income exemption for each paycheck. This comes from the W-4 form that you filled out when you were hired. Remember a few paragraphs ago I mentioned that we would be taking one exemption. So, the number of exemptions for this example is 1. And from the table each exemption is $4000 annually. But we have 26 pay periods, so the deduction per period is $4000/26 or $153.85. This is very important for our calculation as you will see.
4. Add up your "pre-tax" deductions, including 401K, flexible spending contributions, etc. for each pay period. In our example we have no "pre-tax" deductions.
5. Figure out your taxable income for the pay period. In our example, the taxable income will be $2000 - $153.85 or 1846.15 (taxable income = gross pay – exemptions – pretax deductions).
6. Find out and calculate your taxes from the table. For our example – we use TABLE 2 - Biweekly Payroll Period – section (a) Single person. **Note on line 3 of the section (a) table** – the income falls in this range – more than $1529 but less than $3579. Note that the tax calculation is $198.40 + 25% of everything over $1529. Here is that calculation:

$1846.15 – $1529 = 317.15 x .25 = $79.29
Add $79.29 + 198.40 = **$277.69** is the total income tax withholding for the period for this single person who makes $2,000 every two weeks.

Now let's add up our deductions:
Federal Income Tax = **$277.69**
Social Security Tax = **$124**
Medicare Tax = **$29**
Total Taxes = **$430.69**

Since you have had no other deductions – and we will say there live in Nevada or another state that has no state income tax – so your Net Pay will be: **$2,000 - $430.69 = $1,569.31**
**(The tax tables for 2015 follow)**

# Tables for Percentage Method of Withholding
(For Wages Paid in 2015)

**The following payroll tax rates tables are from IRS Notice 1036. The tables include federal withholding for year 2015 (income tax), FICA tax, Medicare tax and FUTA taxes.**

| Tax | Maximum Earnings | Rate |
|---|---|---|
| Social Security Tax | $118,500.00 | 6.20% for the employee and 6.2% for employer |
| Medicare | Unlimited | 1.45% for employee and employer |
| | over $200,000 | Additional 0.9% for the part in excess of $200,000 in a calendar year. Employee only. |

**Deductions per dependent: $4,000.00 (annually)**

## Table 1 -- Year 2015 Federal Income Tax Withholding Weekly Payroll Period

## Table 1 -- Weekly Payroll Period

**(a) SINGLE person** (including head of household) --

| If the amount of wages (after subtracting withholding allowances) is: | | The amount of income tax to withhold is: | |
|---|---|---|---|
| Not over $44.00....... | | $0 | |
| Over -- | But no over -- | | Of excess over -- |
| $44.00 | $222.00 ... | 10% | $44.00 |

| Over -- | But no over -- | | Of excess over -- |
|---|---|---|---|
| $222.00 | $764.00 | ... $17.80 plus 15% | $222.00 |
| $764.00 | $1,789.00 | ... $99.10 plus 25% | $764.00 |
| $1,789.00 | $3,685.00 | ... $355.35 plus 28% | $1,789.00 |
| $3,685.00 | $7,958.00 | ... $886.23 plus 33% | $3,685.00 |
| $7,958.00 | $7,990.00 | ... $2,296.32 plus 35% | $7,958.00 |
| $7,990.00 | ... | ... $2,307.52 plus 39.6% | $7,990.00 |

**(b) Married person --**

If the amount of wages(after subtracting withholding allowances) is:

Not over $165.00.......

The amount of income tax to withhold is:

$0

| Over -- | But no over -- | | Of excess over -- |
|---|---|---|---|
| $165.00 | $520.00 | ... 10% | $165.00 |
| $520.00 | $1,606.00 | ... $35.50 plus 15% | $520.00 |
| $1,606.00 | $3,073.00 | ... $198.40 plus 25% | $1,606.00 |
| $3,073.00 | $4,597.00 | ... $565.15 plus 28% | $3,073.00 |
| $4,597.00 | $8,079.00 | ... $991.87 plus 33% | $4,597.00 |
| $8,079.00 | $9,105.00 | ... $2,140.93 plus 35% | $8,079.00 |
| $9,105.00 | ... | ... $2,500.03 plus 39.6% | $9,105.00 |

# Table 2 -- Biweekly Payroll Period

**(a) SINGLE person** (including head of household) --

If the amount of wages (after subtracting withholding allowances) is:

Not over $88.00.......

The amount of income tax to withhold is:

$0

| Over -- | But no over -- | | Of excess over -- |
|---|---|---|---|
| $88.00 | $443.00 | ... 10% | $88.00 |
| $443.00 | $1,529.00 | ... $35.50 plus 15% | $443.00 |
| $1,529.00 | $3,579.00 | ... $198.40 plus 25% | $1,529.00 |
| $3,579.00 | $7,369.00 | ... $710.90 plus 28% | $3,579.00 |
| $7,369.00 | $15,915.00 | ... $1,772.10 plus 33% | $7,369.00 |
| $15,915.00 | $15,981.00 | ... $4,592.28 plus 35% | $15,915.00 |

| $15,981.00 | ... ... $4,615.38 plus 39.6% | $15,981.00 |

**(b) Married person --**

| If the amount of wages(after subtracting withholding allowances) is: | The amount of income tax to withhold is: |
| Not over $331.00....... | $0 |

| Over -- | But no over -- | | Of excess over -- |
| --- | --- | --- | --- |
| $331.00 | $1,040.00 ... 10% | | $331.00 |
| $1,040.00 | $3,212.00 ... $70.90 plus 15% | | $1,040.00 |
| $3,212.00 | $6,146.00 ... $396.70 plus 25% | | $3,212.00 |
| $6,146.00 | $9,194.00 ... $1,130.20 plus 28% | | $6,146.00 |
| $9,194.00 | $16,158.00 ... $1,983.64 plus 33% | | $9,194.00 |
| $16,158.00 | $18,210.00 ... $4,281.76 plus 35% | | $16,158.00 |
| $18,210.00 | ... ... $4,999.96 plus 39.6% | | $18,210.00 |

# Table 3 -- Semimonthly Payroll Period

**(a) SINGLE person** (including head of household) --

| If the amount of wages (after subtracting withholding allowances) is: | The amount of income tax to withhold is: |
| Not over $96.00....... | $0 |

| Over -- | But no over -- | | Of excess over -- |
| --- | --- | --- | --- |
| $96.00 | $480.00 ... 10% | | $96.00 |
| $480.00 | $1,656.00 ... $38.40 plus 15% | | $480.00 |
| $1,656.00 | $3,877.00 ... $214.80 plus 25% | | $1,656.00 |
| $3,877.00 | $7,983.00 ... $770.05 plus 28% | | $3,877.00 |
| $7,983.00 | $17,242.00 ... $1,919.73 plus 33% | | $7,983.00 |
| $17,242.00 | $17,313.00 ... $4,975.20 plus 35% | | $17,242.00 |
| $17,313.00 | ... ... $5,000.05 plus 39.6% | | $17,313.00 |

**(b) Married person --**

| If the amount of wages (after subtracting withholding allowances) is: | The amount of income tax to withhold is: |

Not over $358.00.......                                  $0

| Over -- | But no over -- | | Of excess over -- |
|---|---|---|---|
| $358.00 | $1,127.00 | ... 10% | $358.00 |
| $1,127.00 | $3,479.00 | ... $76.90 plus 15% | $1,127.00 |
| $3,479.00 | $6,658.00 | ... $429.70 plus 25% | $3,479.00 |
| $6,658.00 | $9,960.00 | ... $1,224.45 plus 28% | $6,658.00 |
| $9,960.00 | $17,504.00 | ... $2,149.01 plus 33% | $9,960.00 |
| $17,504.00 | $19,727.00 | ... $4,638.53 plus 35% | $17,504.00 |
| $19,727.00 | | ... ... $5,416.58 plus 39.6% | $19,727.00 |

# Table 4 -- Monthly Payroll Period

**(a) SINGLE person** (including head of household) --

| If the amount of wages (after subtracting withholding allowances) is: | | The amount of income tax to withhold is: |
|---|---|---|
| Not over $192.00....... | | $0 |

| Over -- | But no over -- | | Of excess over -- |
|---|---|---|---|
| $192.00 | $960.00 | ... 10% | $192.00 |
| $960.00 | $3,313.00 | ... $76.80 plus 15% | $960.00 |
| $3,313.00 | $7,754.00 | ... $429.75 plus 25% | $3,313.00 |
| $7,754.00 | $15,967.00 | ... $1,540.00 plus 28% | $7,754.00 |
| $15,967.00 | $34,483.00 | ... $3,839.64 plus 33% | $15,967.00 |
| $34,483.00 | $34,625.00 | ... $9,949.92 plus 35% | $34,483.00 |
| $34,625.00 | | ... ... $9,999.62 plus 39.6% | $34,625.00 |

**(b) Married person** --

| If the amount of wages (after subtracting withholding allowances) is: | | The amount of income tax to withhold is: |
|---|---|---|
| Not over $717.00....... | | $0 |

| Over -- | But no over -- | | Of excess over -- |
|---|---|---|---|
| $717.00 | $2,254.00 | ... 10% | $717.00 |
| $2,254.00 | $6,958.00 | ... $153.70 plus 15% | $2,254.00 |
| $6,958.00 | $13,317.00 | ... $859.30 plus 25% | $6,958.00 |

| $13,317.00 | $19,921.00 ... $2,449.05 plus 28% | $13,317.00 |
| $19,921.00 | $35,008.00 ... $4,298.17 plus 33% | $19,921.00 |
| $35,008.00 | $39,454.00 ... $9,276.88 plus 35% | $35,008.00 |
| $39,454.00 | ... ... $10,832.98 plus 39.6% | $39,454.00 |

# Table 5 -- Daily or Miscellaneous Payroll Period

**(a) SINGLE person** (including head of household) --

| If the amount of wages (after subtracting withholding allowances) is: | The amount of income tax to withhold is: |
| --- | --- |
| Not over $8.80....... | $0 |

| Over -- | But no over -- | | Of excess over -- |
| --- | --- | --- | --- |
| $8.80 | $44.30 ... 10% | | $8.80 |
| $44.30 | $152.90 ... $3.55 plus 15% | | $44.30 |
| $152.90 | $357.90 ... $19.84 plus 25% | | $152.90 |
| $357.90 | $736.90 ... $71.09 plus 28% | | $357.90 |
| $736.90 | $1,591.50 ... $177.21 plus 33% | | $736.90 |
| $1,591.50 | $1,598.10 ... $459.23 plus 35% | | $1,591.50 |
| $1,598.10 | ... ... $461.54 plus 39.6% | | $1,598.10 |

**(b) Married person** --

| If the amount of wages (after subtracting withholding allowances) is: | The amount of income tax to withhold is: |
| --- | --- |
| Not over $33.10....... | $0 |

| Over -- | But no over -- | | Of excess over -- |
| --- | --- | --- | --- |
| $33.10 | $104.00 ... 10% | | $33.10 |
| $104.00 | $321.20 ... $7.09 plus 15% | | $104.00 |
| $321.20 | $614.60 ... $39.67 plus 25% | | $321.20 |
| $614.60 | $919.40 ... $113.02 plus 28% | | $614.60 |
| $919.40 | $1,615.80 ... $198.36 plus 33% | | $919.40 |
| $1,615.80 | $1,821.00 ... $428.17 plus 35% | | $1,615.80 |
| $1,821.00 | ... ... $499.99 plus 39.6% | | $1,821.00 |

So now that we have explained that complicated mess – I would like you to think why I went through this whole explanation. Because by having the knowledge of why and how much income taxes affect your paycheck – you now can take better control of the process. How? Well that is a great question.

When you are hired, there is a document called a W-4 that you complete to tell the payroll department how many exemptions you are allowed. Remember when we did the payroll income tax deduction calculation and we needed to know how many exemptions the person had indicated they were going to take. This is the document that is used to tell the payroll department what that number is.

As you will see from the document (see next page) it is somewhat complicated, although, to the government's credit, they have tried to make it easier. Essentially, it is based upon how many exemptions you will take when you file your income tax return at the end of the year. Here is the key – just because you have only one child yourself and your wife or husband does not mean that you are limited to only take 3 exemptions. By law, that is how many you will take when you do your income tax. If you take fewer exemptions more will be withheld from your paycheck probably resulting in a larger refund at the end of the year.

This is a very important concept. If you claim a 0 or a 1 on this form because you know that the government will take more withholding – you will probably get a large refund at the end of the year. In this case, you are using the government to act like a forced savings account – so that you can enjoy a large $1000 or $5000 tax refund to spend next year. However, by properly claiming more exemptions per paycheck you would have less money withheld and would have more money to spend throughout the year.

## Form W-4 (2015)

**Purpose.** Complete Form W-4 so that your employer can withhold the correct federal income tax from your pay. Consider completing a new Form W-4 each year and when your personal or financial situation changes.

**Exemption from withholding.** If you are exempt, complete only lines 1, 2, 3, 4, and 7 and sign the form to validate it. Your exemption for 2015 expires February 16, 2016. See Pub. 505, Tax Withholding and Estimated Tax.

**Note.** If another person can claim you as a dependent on his or her tax return, you cannot claim exemption from withholding if your income exceeds $1,050 and includes more than $350 of unearned income (for example, interest and dividends).

**Exceptions.** An employee may be able to claim exemption from withholding even if the employee is a dependent, if the employee:

• is age 65 or older,

• is blind, or

• Will claim adjustments to income; tax credits; or itemized deductions, on his or her tax return.

The exceptions do not apply to supplemental wages greater than $1,000,000.

**Basic instructions.** If you are not exempt, complete the Personal Allowances Worksheet below. The worksheets on page 2 further adjust your withholding allowances based on itemized deductions, certain credits, adjustments to income, or two-earners/multiple jobs situations.

Complete all worksheets that apply. However, you may claim fewer (or zero) allowances. For regular wages, withholding must be based on allowances you claimed and may not be a flat amount or percentage of wages.

**Head of household.** Generally, you can claim head of household filing status on your tax return only if you are unmarried and pay more than 50% of the costs of keeping up a home for yourself and your dependent(s) or other qualifying individuals. See Pub. 501, Exemptions, Standard Deduction, and Filing Information, for information.

**Tax credits.** You can take projected tax credits into account in figuring your allowable number of withholding allowances. Credits for child or dependent care expenses and the child tax credit may be claimed using the Personal Allowances Worksheet below. See Pub. 505 for information on converting your other credits into withholding allowances.

**Nonwage income.** If you have a large amount of nonwage income, such as interest or dividends, consider making estimated tax payments using Form 1040-ES, Estimated Tax for Individuals. Otherwise, you may owe additional tax. If you have pension or annuity income, see Pub. 505 to find out if you should adjust your withholding on Form W-4 or W-4P.

**Two earners or multiple jobs.** If you have a working spouse or more than one job, figure the total number of allowances you are entitled to claim on all jobs using worksheets from only one Form W-4. Your withholding usually will be most accurate when all allowances are claimed on the Form W-4 for the highest paying job and zero allowances are claimed on the others. See Pub. 505 for details.

**Nonresident alien.** If you are a nonresident alien, see Notice 1392, Supplemental Form W-4 Instructions for Nonresident Aliens, before completing this form.

**Check your withholding.** After your Form W-4 takes effect, use Pub. 505 to see how the amount you are having withheld compares to your projected total tax for 2015. See Pub. 505, especially if your earnings exceed $130,000 (Single) or $180,000 (Married).

**Future developments.** Information about any future developments affecting Form W-4 (such as legislation enacted after we release it) will be posted at www.irs.gov/w4.

---

### Personal Allowances Worksheet (Keep for your records.)

A  Enter "1" for **yourself** if no one else can claim you as a dependent . . . . . . . . . . . . **A** _____

B  Enter "1" if:
  • You are single and have only one job; or
  • You are married, have only one job, and your spouse does not work; or
  • Your wages from a second job or your spouse's wages (or the total of both) are $1,500 or less. } . . . **B** _____

C  Enter "1" for your **spouse**. But, you may choose to enter "-0-" if you are married and have either a working spouse or more than one job. (Entering "-0-" may help you avoid having too little tax withheld.) . . . . . . . . . **C** _____

D  Enter number of **dependents** (other than your spouse or yourself) you will claim on your tax return . . . . . . . **D** _____

E  Enter "1" if you will file as **head of household** on your tax return (see conditions under **Head of household** above) . . **E** _____

F  Enter "1" if you have at least $2,000 of **child or dependent care expenses** for which you plan to claim a credit . . . **F** _____
  (**Note.** Do **not** include child support payments. See Pub. 503, Child and Dependent Care Expenses, for details.)

G  **Child Tax Credit** (including additional child tax credit). See Pub. 972, Child Tax Credit, for more information.
  • If your total income will be less than $65,000 ($100,000 if married), enter "2" for each eligible child; then **less** "1" if you have two to four eligible children or **less** "2" if you have five or more eligible children.
  • If your total income will be between $65,000 and $84,000 ($100,000 and $119,000 if married), enter "1" for each eligible child . . . **G** _____

H  Add lines A through G and enter total here. (**Note.** This may be different from the number of exemptions you claim on your tax return.) ▶ **H** _____

For accuracy, complete all worksheets that apply.
  • If you plan to **itemize** or **claim adjustments to income** and want to reduce your withholding, see the **Deductions and Adjustments Worksheet** on page 2.
  • If you are **single and have more than one job** or are **married and you and your spouse both work** and the combined earnings from all jobs exceed $50,000 ($20,000 if married), see the **Two-Earners/Multiple Jobs Worksheet** on page 2 to avoid having too little tax withheld.
  • If **neither** of the above situations applies, **stop here** and enter the number from line H on line 5 of Form W-4 below.

-------- Separate here and give Form W-4 to your employer. Keep the top part for your records. --------

| Form **W-4** Department of the Treasury Internal Revenue Service | **Employee's Withholding Allowance Certificate** ▶ Whether you are entitled to claim a certain number of allowances or exemption from withholding is subject to review by the IRS. Your employer may be required to send a copy of this form to the IRS. | OMB No. 1545-0074 20**15** |
|---|---|---|
| 1  Your first name and middle initial    Last name | | 2  Your social security number |
| Home address (number and street or rural route) | 3 ☐ Single  ☐ Married  ☐ Married, but withhold at higher Single rate. Note. If married, but legally separated, or spouse is a nonresident alien, check the "Single" box. | |
| City or town, state, and ZIP code | 4  If your last name differs from that shown on your social security card, check here. You must call 1-800-772-1213 for a replacement card. ▶ ☐ | |

5  Total number of allowances you are claiming (from line **H** above **or** from the applicable worksheet on page 2)  **5** _____

6  Additional amount, if any, you want withheld from each paycheck . . . . . . . . . . . . . **6** $ _____

7  I claim exemption from withholding for 2015, and I certify that I meet **both** of the following conditions for exemption.
  • Last year I had a right to a refund of **all** federal income tax withheld because I had **no** tax liability, **and**
  • This year I expect a refund of **all** federal income tax withheld because I expect to have **no** tax liability.
  If you meet both conditions, write "Exempt" here . . . . . . . . . . . . . . . ▶ **7** _____

Under penalties of perjury, I declare that I have examined this certificate and, to the best of my knowledge and belief, it is true, correct, and complete.

Employee's signature
(This form is not valid unless you sign it.) ▶ _____  Date ▶ _____

| 8  Employer's name and address (Employer: Complete lines 8 and 10 only if sending to the IRS.) | 9 Office code (optional) | 10  Employer identification number (EIN) |
|---|---|---|

For Privacy Act and Paperwork Reduction Act Notice, see page 2.    Cat. No. 10220Q    Form **W-4** (2015)

Think about this.  By allowing the government to over withhold more money each week, you are in essence giving the government a tax-free, interest-free loan for them to do whatever they want, for the whole year just so they can pay it back to you next year.  Does that make sense??  Remember the three lessons from Chapter 1 -

1.  Present money is ALWAYS worth more than future money.  Money I have in my hands right now is worth more than a future promise of money.  The reason: Money I have now is worth what it is worth RIGHT NOW – future money is basically worth less because it is NOT, and never can be, 100% guaranteed.

2.  For the privilege to spend somebody else's present money with a payment of your future money, it costs you interest or a fee or some other cost above and beyond your future money since, (see #1), future money is worth less than present money.

3.  While we never pay interest or fees when we are kids, in the real world no one is going to give you present money to spend today for the cost of just your future promise of money in the future.  (There are rare exceptions to this with cars being sold for 0% financing – but take my word for it, if you miss one payment – it is no longer free).

So why would you allow the government to have your present money – which is worth more to you now than the future promise of the exact same amount of money back to you next year – AND allow them to have it for free --- with no interest or payment to you?

Although you may argue that you like that large refund for a vacation or other large purchase, why not consider putting that little bit of extra money ***every pay check,*** into a savings account (any maybe earn a little interest), or even spend it now?  Here are two things to consider:

1.  If the tax refund you received at the end of the year was more than $1000, and you are paid bi-weekly, that means you could have had $38.46 more every paycheck.  Could you have used that money over the course of the year?

2.  Second, if I wanted you to loan me $38.46 every time you got paid – and in return I would give you $1000 next year and not charge me a penny for doing it – would you take that deal?  Seriously – would just give someone $38.46 every time you got paid just so you could get a $1000 check next year??  Well that is EXACTLY what you are doing with the IRS.  You are giving them a tax-free, interest-free loan of your money – which you could have throughout the year.

The other reason people do this is because they do not want to owe the IRS at the end of the year.  But by planning and doing the math for the whole year, you will be able to determine what you will pay the IRS and what you will owe the IRS and should be able to know exactly how much you want taken from your check.  It is financially worth the effort to do this calculation.  Remember, you can change your W-4 as often as you like during the year.  If you expect a bonus or to get a raise, or work fewer hours, always consider recalculating the W-4 to get a more realistic picture of what you will owe the IRS for the year.  Then alter your withholding accordingly.

Look over that W-4 form again. The way to control what is taken from your check is in line 5 and line 6. In the calculations above ending in item H, the number derived is the true number you are allowed to take and should take based upon normal circumstances. However, if you know you owed the IRS money last year, you can claim a lower number in line 5. On the other hand, if you had a large refund from the government last year, you can claim a larger number. Additionally, if you know that you will get all the money back that the government is going to take you can write "EXEMPT" on line 7 and there will be no federal income tax taken from your check. However, it is important to remember that if you have too little taken and owe the IRS at the end of the year (more than $600), they will assess a penalty for having "too little" withheld from your paycheck. This is the reason many people don't play around with this because they are afraid of owing a penalty.

The goal is to calculate this as accurately as possible so that you break even and don't overpay or underpay the government. To do yourself a good service, it is best if you perform an estimated tax return every month throughout the year to see how you stand. What you say? You can actually do this? Well, the answer is yes – and not only yes – but positively yes. By doing this you prevent any unpleasant surprise at the end of the year (like owing a lot to the IRS) or you can alter you plans to get more on your weekly paycheck (and avoid a large tax free loan of your money to the government).

So how do we do this? You can use a spreadsheet to do a mock tax return – similar to the one I have here (see next page). Using the example, we used to calculate the payroll withholding, I can do an estimated tax return for our single worker.

## 2015 Estimated Taxes

| | | |
|---|---|---|
| 7 | Wages | $52,000.00 |
| 8 | Interest | |
| 12 | | |
| 13 | Capital Gain | $250.00 |
| 15 | IRA Distribution | $0.00 |
| 19 | Retirement Income | |
| 21 | Other Inc. (Gamb Win) | $1,500.00 |
| 22 | SUBTOTAL | $53,750.00 |
| 27 | | |
| | IRA Contributions | -$1,000.00 |
| 29 | | |
| 37 | Subtotal | $52,750.00 |
| 40 | Itemized Deduct | -$10,747.00 |
| 42 | Exemptions | -$4,000.00 |
| 43 | Taxable Income | $38,003.00 |
| 44 | Tax | $5,294.50 |
| 60 | Total Tax | $5,294.50 |
| 61 | Withheld | $7,219.94 |
| 62 | Estimated Payments | |
| 72 | Payments | $7,219.94 |
| 73 or | Line 60- Line72 | -$1,925.44 |

2015 Ordinary Tax Rates for Single Filing Status
[Tax Rate Schedule X, Internal Revenue Code section 1(c)]

| If taxable income is | | a | b | c |
|---|---|---|---|---|
| over | but not | Minus | Multiplication | Additional |
| $0 | $9,225 | $0 | × 10% | $0 |
| 9,225 | 37,450 | 9,225 | × 15% | 922.5 |
| 37,450 | 90,750 | 37,450 | × 25% | 5,156.25 |
| 90,750 | 189,300 | 90,750 | × 28% | 18,481.25 |
| 189,300 | 411,500 | 189,300 | × 33% | 46,075.25 |
| 411,500 | 413,200 | 411,500 | × 35% | 119,401.25 |
| 413,200 | -- | 413,200 | × 39.6% | 119,996.25 |

| Mort | RE | Sales | Car Prop | Donations | Gam Loss |
|---|---|---|---|---|---|
| 8000 | 800 | 400 | 247 | 500 | 800 |

In our example, I have made a couple of assumptions. Here they are:

1. This year our single person received his normal paychecks (26 in all).
2. As in the initial example, he had one exemption so the federal taxes taken out were $277.69 per paycheck.
3. He had a $250 capital gain on the sale of some stock.
4. He won $1500 on a visit to casino and received a W-2G from the casino.
5. He made a $1,000 contribution to his IRA that he has
6. He itemizes deductions and has $8000 in mortgage interest, $800 in real estate taxes, $400 in sales taxes, $247 in personal property taxes, $500 in cash donations to the church, and $800 in gambling losses to offset the $1500 win.

As you can see from the spreadsheet, I have made a mock tax return that is based on the information he knows at this point in time, and most of the items are estimates for the entire year. As the year progresses, he can make the estimates closer to what the actual figures are. What he can notice at this point in time (let's assume it is the month of June) is that he is expecting to receive a $1925 refund. Now, he has read this book and he prefers to have more money in his pocket than to give the IRS an interest-free loan. So, he has decided to go to his employer and ask to re-do his W-4. Since half the year is gone, and since there are only 13 paychecks left, he will change the form to get more per paycheck. He has already had $277.69 x 13 or $3,609.97 withheld. So, if we take that projected refund of 1925 and divide it by the remaining 13 checks – he can technically have $148 less taken out in taxes for the remainder of the year and he will still have had enough withholding taken to meet his tax obligation. To show this here is the math:

- 3,606.97 already taken
- 13 check remaining and $277.69 will be taken out if no change to W-4
- Change W-4 so that only $129.69 is taken instead of $277.69 (277.69 – 148)
- 13 checks at $129.69 = $1,685.97
- 1,685.97 + 3606.97 = $5,292.94 leaving a potential refund of 44 cents.

AND – best of all – he gets $148 more per paycheck for the rest of the year to do whatever he wants.

In retrospect, it really is about each person's personal preference with respect to how they handle their money. I know there are people who will say – "I like having a large refund so that I can buy a vacation or something nice." But for me, I say, instead – why don't you take that little bit of extra money *every pay check,* place it in a savings account (any maybe earn a little interest), or even spend it now? If you still want to go on that government refund vacation – get the money now –save it in savings account and you still will have the same amount come February of the next year. Additionally, if you decide you would rather buy something instead of going on the vacation – you will have additional money in your paycheck every pay period to do what you want. Call it what you may – I think placing yourself in control of the money is better than giving it to the government as an interest- free loan.

*(Note on this chapter – this chapter was written in 2015, but the principles and concepts shown still apply. Use the tax tables for*

*the year you want to estimate – and model the estimated taxes spreadsheet to the tax form for the year you want.)*

# Chapter 7
# Bank Fees

Another area where consumers can have a lot of control but most don't use the control is the area of bank fees.

Let's face it. Banks offer many services and most of us utilize a bank (or credit union) to handle most of our day to day financial transactions. The most common product we use from a bank is a checking account. We generally have our payroll check directly deposited into our account and then, by either debit card transactions, ATM transactions, electronic payment services or via writing checks, utilize the bank to pay for our expenditures.

While an important item for the bank's deposit base, checking accounts are not products where the bank makes their most money. In fact, years ago, free checking accounts were offered and banks actually looked upon checking accounts as loss leaders for other banking business. Checking accounts are a lot of work for a bank with little revenue generation. They are not a reason that a bank is in business.

Banks make money by making loans – plain and simple. They need deposits (hence the reason they want checking accounts) and then take this money that they have on deposit and lend it out. They make their most money on the "interest spread" – the difference in the amount of interest they pay for the deposits vs.

the amount of interest they charge for all the loans. They pay little, if any, interest on the checking account deposit money, so the spread is bigger (again the reason why they desire checking accounts).

But, as mentioned, checking accounts cost a lot in terms of transaction processing, labor costs, other services, etc. In fact, in the past 5 years, the reason banks have raised the fees they charge for checking accounts is to try to recoup all the costs associated with having those accounts.

The bank's objective is to maximize fee revenue from you. On the other hand, your objective should be to minimize bank fees charged to you. The following information will help save you from falling into the "bank fee" traps that cost you money.

Bank fees for checking accounts have dramatically risen in the past 5 years. No longer can you find a "free" checking account – and if you do – it is probably because you are either a long time customer, a protected senior citizen, a young adult starting out, you keep enough money on deposit for the bank to keep them from charging a fee, or you have a large relationship with bank (have several products with them). Typically, you will probably note many of the following fees:

- Monthly maintenance fee
- A paper statement fee
- ATM "out-of-network" fees (charged by both the issuing and receiving banks)
- Check writing fee (a fee for writing a check)
- Replacement ATM fee
- Check Image service fee
- Overdraft fees

- NSF fees
- Overdraft protection fee
- Overdraft transfer fee
- Inter-account transfer fee
- Electronic Payment fees (ACH, wire-transfers, or other e-banking fees)
- Stop payment fee
- Direct deposit fee

Each year I am amazed that the banks seem to come up with some other bizarre fee. To prevent being charged these fees you must be diligent and know how the bank utilizes your personal consumer behavior and your need or want for convenience to take advantage by charging you a fee. If you know the "bank fee traps" you can learn to avoid them and minimize fees.

Probably the most expensive fee is the Overdraft fee. To the bank, an overdraft is short-term loan. You, for whatever reason, have spent more than you had in your checking account (or you tried to pull a fast one and wrote a check that you thought would not clear your account until you deposited more money). The bank, has fronted you some money to cover the expense that you have incurred and caused your account to go negative. This is bank trap fee "numero uno"!

Overdraft fees are usually around $27 to $35 despite the fact that you may have overdrawn only a little. Think about this – if you have overdrawn your account by $35 and the fee is $35, the bank has just made more than 100% interest on your absent-mindedness. To avoid this fee, balance your account (see chapter 3) and make sure you have enough money in your account to cover all your expenditures. Remember, it's up to you to be financially responsible and if you don't and make a mistake, the bank will usually make you pay.

Because banks know that individual's spending habits can sometimes get out of control, or because individuals are not as responsible as they should be – this is why this fee is there – and it is one they rely on the most to make a lot of revenue for the bank. This is one bank fee trap you need to avoid like the plague. Really – just don't let it happen.

The next bank fee that drives me crazy is the bank ATM fee. Banks provide ATMs so that you can withdraw cash, at your convenience, from many places throughout the world without having to make a visit to the bank. (Now remember – it is your money to begin with). Each bank has paid a substantial amount of money to place one of these teller-replacement machines in strategic places throughout the city or state so that you can access your own money. This is a great idea, right?

Well that is until you decide to use an ATM that is one your bank does not own or is not in their "network". (Without getting too complicated, their network is the transaction processor that they contract with to collect the electronic transmission from). When you use an out-of-network ATM, there is a convenience charge for using that ATM – despite the fact that it dispenses money anyway and despite the fact that you are trying to access your own money! This fee is for allowing you the convenience of using that ATM at that particular place that just happens not to be in your bank's network. The fee is usually about $2; which for most folks is probably not too bad – except that the fee is actually the fee charged by the bank that owns that ATM. So that fee gets passed onto you. In turn, your bank also charges you a fee for accessing your own money from an ATM that is not in their network and that fee is usually about $2 or $3 as well. So, for the convenience of accessing your own money from a teller machine that just happens to be close to where you are at any point in time – you have to pay a total of about $5 in fees. Now, just think – if you do this three times a week – that could be $15 in fees a week. And if you do this almost every week – let's say 45 out of 52 weeks that would be $15 x45 or $675 in ATM fees!

There is $675 you are just giving to the banks – for free – just because you don't want to make the effort to make sure you are accessing an ATM that is in your bank's network. Really – is that a smart way to handle your money? Couldn't you use the $675 to do something else instead of just giving it to the bank?

Another fee that people just don't really think about is a check-writing fee. For accounts where you need to maintain a very low balance, banks have decided that since you are a little higher risk, they charge you a small fee to write a check. Really? Charge you a fee to spend you own money? Yep, it is true – some banks will charge you a 10 cents or 15 cents fee to write a check. In today's electronic environment, this is probably not a big deal since you probably don't write that many checks. But if you write 10 checks a month and the fee is 10 cents, it's another miscellaneous dollar you are giving away to the bank.

Another fee is the infamous Monthly Maintenance fee. This fee is one I really dislike. Because banks were losing money on checking accounts, they started to charge a monthly maintenance fee to you just for having your checking account. When this started to occur, I went immediately to my bank and stated I wanted to close my account. I refuse to pay a monthly maintenance fee. Luckily, I had been a customer for many years, I had direct deposit into my account, and I had a savings account with them. So, all they did is ask me to make at least one automated transfer from my checking account to my saving account – and they would waive the fee. So, each month, I have $50 automatically transferred from my checking account to my savings account and I avoid the $6.95 monthly maintenance fee. This was a good deal because it also made me save $50 a month.

Paying a monthly maintenance fee is something you should try to avoid. While banks will say it is necessary because of increased costs – whether you have an account with them or not – they still process and do the same amount of work they did in the past when there was no fee. Work with your bank to get this fee waived. As I mentioned, I was able to have my fee waived because I had been a customer for many years, had my paycheck directly deposited and maintained a saving account with the bank. The bank asked me to make at least one automated transfer from checking to savings each month. By transferring $50 per month from checking to savings, I avoided the monthly maintenance fee. See if you can do that as well.

Here are a few other miscellaneous fees I would like to address:
- Replacement ATM fee – Because you have accidentally lost you ATM or debit card, the bank believes they should charge you $5. The ATM card is a card you get so that you have the ability to access your money from an automated teller (i.e., you are already saving the bank money since they can hire one less teller). Why should have to pay them an additional $5 just because you lose the card. Tell the bank you will bank somewhere else. Be firm – but understand – banks make a lot of money on fees and they will not easily back down on fees.

- Electronic Payment or Deposit Fees – When electronic banking came out, banks thought it would be a wonderful idea to charge a little something, like a nickel or a dime, for any kind of electronic payment or automated deposit. People revolted and most banks now offer free electronic deposits and free electronic payments. If your bank charges for e-banking transactions – ditch them.

- Paper Statement Fee – to persuade more consumers to do electronic banking, many banks have now asked their customers to get electronic statements. Not a bad thing, it's environmentally friendly and it makes sense. But I believe they crossed the line when they decided for those older customers and/or people who were not paying attention, they would start charging a $1 or $2 free for receiving a paper statement. If your bank charges this fee, ask them how you can stop it and opt out of the paper statement. Signing up for an electronic statement is easy and worth the effort.

So now that I have gone over many of the most avoidable fees, let's discuss this in a real-life scenario to helps illustrate how you can avoid these fees. Bill, is a single guy in his early 30's, who has been banking with Bank X since he was in college. He started with a student checking account, and, once he graduated, went up another level to their standard checking account and he also opened a small saving account. Bill got his car loan through Bank X and, plans to stay with Bank X despite that fact that, like most other major banks, their fees have been increasing.

Bill has been reading the drafts of this book and, coincidentally, received a paper statement in the mail for his bank account with

Bank X. He starts to analyze the statement. He is surprised to see a number of fees:

- First, there is the monthly service fee of $7. This was instituted by his bank about a year ago and he didn't think anything about at the time. But now he is beginning to think it is a little expensive to pay the bank $7 every month just to have a checking account.

- Next, he sees that his bank has charged him $2 for the paper statement. See, the bank sent him a notice about a year ago stating that everyone should sign up for an electronic statement – but he never did. Since he did not sign up, they still send the paper statement – for the $2 per month cost.

- Next, he sees that he wrote 15 checks this month. What he did not realize is that his bank instituted a check writing fee since they wanted everyone to start using electronic banking. The fee kicks in after the first 5 hand written checks. Since he had 15 checks, 10 of those cost him 10 cents each to write. Another $1 fee.

- He now also sees that, as he usually does every month, he forgot that his automatic car payment comes out on the 14$^{th}$ of the month – and he gets paid on the 15$^{th}$. Even though he could have changed the date of that payment, he never did – and it almost always overdraws his account for that one day. The cost for the overdraft is $35.

- He then looks to see that he took money from the ATM right in his office lobby 8 times. Well, that ATM is not in his bank's network so there was a $2 charge from that bank every time he took the money. Additionally, his bank charges him an additional $2.50 for each time he takes money from an ATM not in their network. 8 x (2 +2.50) = 8 x 4.50 = $36 in ATM fees.

- Next, he notices that his sister, who lives across town, sends him an electronic payment every month for the money she owes him – and this particular deposit to his account costs him a $3 e-deposit fee due to the way she does the electronic deposit.

- Finally, he lost his ATM card and the bank charged him a $5 replacement fee for that new ATM card.

The total bank fees for the month: 7 +2 +1 +35 +36 +3 +5 = $89 in bank fees for the month. Additionally, except for the $5 ATM replacement fee, most of these are recurring every month – so his total yearly projected bank fees for this year are $84 x 12 = $1,008 + the $5 replacement card fee or $1,013.

Now think of this. Bill is just one consumer. What if there are about 10,000 people who are just like Bill and the bank is making the same amount of fee income on them. That's $10 million in free fee income for the bank!

So, after consulting with me, we made a few minor changes in Bill's behavior and did the following:

- First, we went to his bank and inquired about the type of checking accounts they had. We were able to determine that he had a basic account – but since he had been with the bank a number of years, they could upgrade him to a tier 2 account, which had a few more perks. One of the perks was that, since he had a savings account, if he allowed the bank to do an automatic savings transfer every month into his savings, he would have the account maintenance fee for his checking account waived. Bill agreed to do it and agreed to have $25 transferred each month from his checking to his savings automatically. This automatic transfer would allow him to no longer have a checking account maintenance fee as long as he maintained both accounts and the transfer.

- Next, I helped Bill setup an online account with the bank and we opted out of the paper statement he was receiving every month. By going paperless, we were going to save him $2 a month.

- Next, with the online account, I assisted him to setup auto-bill pay on a number of accounts and setup electronic payments for many of his bills. By doing this we would cut down the amount of paper checks he was writing to about 2 or 3 a month. No more going over the 5 check writing limit so this would save him on average $1 a month.

- Next, we talked to the bank about his car payment and they agreed to postpone the payment due date for 5 more days – so starting next month they would take the car payment every 19th or 20$^{th}$ of the month instead of the 14$^{th}$. This would help prevent that nasty overdraft fee of $35.

- Next, we found out that an ATM that was in his bank's network was about 2 doors down from his office – so I talked Bill into promising me that he would walk the small 50 foot walk two buildings down and get his ATM cash from that ATM instead of the out-of-network ATM that was in his building's lobby. The extra little walk would do him good -- and – he would save $4.50 every time he went to take cash (averaging about 8 times a month and a savings of $36 on average per month.)

- Next, we called his sister across town and mentioned that her deposit to his account was costing him $3 every time she did it. She was surprised and said she would see if there was another way to pay him with no fee – or she would just write a check. The check would cost her nothing – and she could mail it or just drop it off when she came to see him – which he did not mind because he had not seen her much in the last year and it would be good to see her.

Effectively we eliminated almost all the fees - and his projected bank fee cost for the next 12 months was down to zero! With only a few modest changes in behavior, we were able to save him a projected $1,000 over the course of a year by eliminated pesky bank fees. Could you do the same if you changed a few habits? Take a look at your next statement and see.

The moral of the story is that banks "know" a lot about individual's personal financial habits. They can tell the way many people do things for convenience (like go to the closest ATM, don't change their banking habits, etc.) and use this to their advantage by charging "convenience" fees. Remember in chapter 4 on budgeting where I said you always pay for convenience?

So be vigilant in your quest to eliminate bank fees where you can. If, after trying your hardest, you still feel that you are being "fee-ed" to death – do what many smart consumers do – change banks! After searching, find one that will do the best for your personal situation and minimize the fees they charge you to do so. You will be glad you did – and you will save yourself a little bit of money along the way.

# Chapter 8
# Credit Card Basics

In chapter 1 we talked about children spending their future money (or earnings). Think of credit cards as doing this on steroids.

Most consumers have credit cards and banks love to provide them. We've talked about how banks make their most money – by loaning it out and making interest (more money) on the money they have. Credit cards allow the bank to make loans on money they don't have – and – allow them to make a lot of interest on that money they don't really have! This is pure profit for the bank – and the interest can be very high – 15, 20, 24% or more for those with poor credit or who miss payments. Banks love to give out credit cards and consumers happily use them (or abuse them) because they have a "credit line" to spend.

Most consumers use credit cards for the wrong reasons. When you ask consumers about credit cards their typical answers are:

- "I use it in case of an emergency."
- Or, "if I am short money to pay for something, I place it on a credit card so I can pay for it later."
- Still another – "since I don't make enough money now, I use it to buy necessities until I can get enough money to pay it off."

- Here is one more – "I can buy things that are on sale or clearance and get the item for an exceptional price – I can buy it now at the sale price and save money since I'm getting it at a lower price."

Think about all those statements and the common theme. These consumers have the ability to purchase items, stuff, with future money. As we learned from chapter 1 – future money is never worth what present money is – it is worth less. So, on the surface – this looks great! You are buying something NOW – that will actually cost more - later! Sounds terrific, no?? Well let's look at this a little more closely.

What you are really doing is buying something NOW that you really cannot afford. Regardless of whether it is a better price or not – if you are not paying off your credit card in full every month – you are committing your future earnings to buy something now that you must pay back later - and paying it back later costs more than what you are paying for it now! That cost is the finance charge (or interest if you want to really look it properly) on the money the bank has "loaned" you. That's right – a credit card is nothing more than a short-term (or for many people long-term) loan. And the interest is 10-20%.

Here is another way to look at this: You want to buy something expensive (about $10,000) and do not have the money. A friend says they will give you the money and says he will not charge you any interest. You and he agree that you will pay it back in one year. So, when the year is up, you pay him back $10,000.

Now let's look at the credit card situation. You want to buy $10,000 worth of stuff today and don't have the money. You use your credit card and they only charge you 12% finance charges (or

1% per month). For simplicity, in this example, we will only charge finance charge on the outstanding balance. You make the first payment of $1,000 and the interest for the first month $10000 x .12/12 = $100. Next month, you place nothing else on the card and you pay another $1,000. The interest is $9,000 x .12/12 = $90. If this were to continue for 10 months and you paid it down completed, your total interest charge for the 10 months would be $100 + $90 + $80 + $70 + $60 + $50 + $40... + 10 = $550. So, this is not too bad. But remember – this plan works only if you continue to pay $1,000 every month for the next 10 months – and that you do not place anything else on the credit card. Too many times what really happens in real life is one of the following:

- You can't afford the $1,000 payments one of the months, so you only pay $100. This prolongs the payback period to get the card down to 0.
- You forget to make a payment or are late and the credit card company zaps you will a late fee of $30 and hikes your finance charge rate up to 21%
- You need some more stuff so you decide you will place $3000 worth of more stuff on the credit card and the 3 months of payments you just made have been washed away and your balance is back up to $10,000 after three months and you have paid already $270 in finance charges.
- Or finally, you get your hours cut from your job or lose your job and can't afford to pay $1,000 a month until you find a better job so you pay the minimum payment of $75 and the finance charge is now about $60 so the net amount taken from the outstanding balance is only $15. At this rate you pay this credit card off in about 8 years!

As you can see, this is almost the same situation that we had in chapter 1 about the young child buying things they really could not afford and using their future allowance thinking that they would be all set in 5-10 weeks. The difference here is the situation is magnified at least 100 fold and, worse yet, you are getting charged interest (which you were not when you were a child).

Most people use credit cards to give themselves the ability to purchase items they really cannot afford today for the promise that they will pay it back in the future. Look up the definition of a loan. Does this look familiar?

So, does this mean that a consumer should never use a credit card? Absolute not! Credit cards are a wonderful tool when used correctly and carefully. The key is to pay off your balance EVERY month. If you do this, you are using the bank's money today – and paying it back to them in full – for no interest charge. They are giving you a loan for one month that you are paying back in full. The important thing is to have the discipline to pay it down every month. If you have this discipline – you can reap some very nice benefits. It also has the following significant consumer advantages:

- Good credit to buy a home or car (which is something you really do need to have to obtain a loan)
- You are actually only purchasing items that you know you can afford to pay back in one month. If you need something very expensive that you cannot payback in one month – don't place it on a credit card (you are living within your means and only buying what you can really afford).
- You are keeping yourself as debt-free as possible
- You are using the bank's money – for free – to purchase stuff that you can afford to pay back.

On the other hand, if you know yourself not to have this discipline – then you should probably not use credit cards because you will find yourself in an endless loop of debt. So, if you find yourself in this situation, you need to remember the following things:

- You placed yourself into this situation because you purchased more stuff than you could afford. Plain and simple – you over spent. You need to stop doing that. Learn to control your spending.
- You need to make sure you are making "headway". Paying a minimum balance when the minimum balance is only covering less than half of the finance charge is not going to get you out of the hole. Make sure that the finance charge is less than 20% of your payment. If the finance charge is $30 – your payment needs to be at least $150.
- Consider a debt consolidation loan – particularly if the interest on the loan is less than the percentage on your credit cards. Pay down the credit cards and curb your spending to avoid being right back where you are now later on
- Consider a home equity loan if you have equity in your house. But again – only if you can get a very good interest rate – and throw your credit cards away unless you pay them down every month.

One of the better offers for someone who is drowning in credit card debt – is the balance transfer for 0% for one year. This offer is a wonderful way to pay down your debt – again – if you remain discipline in your payment and spending habits. Let's examine these offers in a more detail.

What banks have done to lure more customers into getting their credit card – is to offer you the ability to "balance transfer" the balance on one or more credit cards and you will have 0% interest for one whole year. The banks hope that you will transfer over a lot of debt, and, after the one-year grace period, will now be their customer paying full interest rate on all that existing debt. They also know that people who have a lot of debt and take them up on this offer, may be the type of person who forgets to make a payment – and in doing so – is required to pay all the past interest that would have been taken if you had opened up a new account with the regular interest rate. Moral of the story – don't ever miss a payment on these special offers!

However, if you have mended your ways and do get one of these offers, they are a very good way to pay down your debt. The fee to do this is usually 3 or 4%, but if the balance you are doing this for will take you more than 3 or 4 payments – it is worth paying the upfront fee. Here are some significant advantages for doing this if you can stay the course:

- All of your payments during the 1-year 0% interest period go to pay down the debt – no interest will be charged on that debt.
- If you make any new purchases – those will be charged finance charges – but it is usually at a much lower rate than your existing credit cards
- By doing this, you are showing all future creditors that you are serious about managing your debt and your credit score will probably rise.

It is important to remember that the goal of these special 0% offers should be for you to manage your debt or get rid of credit card balances completely in the one year or 18-month period. Using it for any other reason than that is just kicking your credit problems down the road further.

Finally, for most people who carry balances, I would like to cover how the banks calculate the finance charge. One would think that this is a very simple task – but it is not. Most banks do follow a process – but it can vary from bank to bank. If you really want to attempt to figure out what your finance charge will be – READ the credit card statement or agreement VERY carefully. By law, they are required to tell you how they calculate the finance charge.

Attached on the next page is a sample excerpt from a credit card statement you would receive when you get your monthly credit card statement. Notice in the area where it says calculation of balances subject to Interest Rate (it can also be called Finance Rate and Finance Charges). Notice in this sample how they calculate your interest. Most, if not all of the credit card companies calculate the finance charge (or interest) using the "Average Daily Balance method." The average daily balance method is one where they will calculate a separate daily balance and apply the daily interest rate (the rate divided by 365 days) and they multiply the rate times the outstanding balance for that day. So if you make purchases and they are applied that day, the purchases would be included in the daily interest calculation for that day, at the end of the day. Additionally, if you made payments or had credits that were applied that day, the calculation of interest for that day would take those into account as well.

As you can see, this can become very complicated. This is the reason banks have computer programs that calculate this every night and keep a running total for your account until the day when the statement closing date comes. Once that day comes, they take the accumulated total and place that on your statement which shows the finance charge for that statement period (or interest).

# Sample Text from Credit Card Statement

## PAYING INTEREST

We will not charge interest on Purchases on the next statement if you pay the New Balance Total in full by the Payment Due Date, and you had paid in full by the previous Payment Due Date. We will begin charging interest on Balance Transfers and Cash Advances on the transaction date.

## CALCULATION OF BALANCES SUBJECT TO INTEREST RATE

Average Daily Balance Method (including new Purchases):

We calculate separate Balances Subject to an Interest Rate for Purchases and for each Introductory or Promotional Offer balance consisting of Purchases. We do this by: (1) calculating a daily balance for each day in the billing cycle; (2) adding all the daily balances together; and (3) dividing the sum of the daily balances by the number of days in the billing cycle.

To calculate the daily balance for each day in this statement's billing cycle, we: (1) take the beginning balance; (2) add an amount equal to the applicable Daily Periodic Rate multiplied by the previous day's daily balance; (3) add new Purchases, new Account Fees, and new Transaction Fees; and (4) subtract applicable payments and credits. If any daily balance is less than zero we treat it as zero.

Average Balance Method (including new Balance Transfers and new Cash Advances).

We calculate separate Balances Subject to an Interest Rate for Balance Transfers, Cash Advances, and for each Introductory or Promotional Offer balance consisting of Balance Transfers or Cash Advances. We do this by: (1) calculating a daily balance for each day in this statement's billing cycle; (2) calculating a daily balance for each day prior to this statement's billing cycle that had a "Pre-Cycle balance" — a Pre-Cycle balance is a Balance Transfer or a Cash Advance with a transaction date prior to this statement's billing cycle but with a posting date within this statement's billing cycle; (3) adding all the daily balances together; and (4) dividing the sum of the daily balances by the number of days in this statement's billing cycle.

To calculate the daily balance for each day in this statement's billing cycle, we: (1) take the beginning balance; (2) add an amount equal to the applicable Daily Periodic Rate multiplied by the previous day's daily balance; (3) add new Balance Transfers, new Cash Advances and Transaction Fees; and (4) subtract applicable payments and credits. If any daily balance is less than zero we treat it as zero.

To calculate a daily balance for each day prior to this statement's billing cycle that had a Pre-Cycle balance: (1) we take the beginning balance attributable solely to Pre-Cycle balance (which will be zero on the transaction date of the first Pre-Cycle balance); (2) add an amount equal to the applicable Daily Periodic Rate multiplied by the previous day's daily balance; (3) and add only the applicable Pre-Cycle balances and their related Transaction Fees. We exclude from this calculation all transactions posted in previous billing cycles.

## PAYMENTS

We credit mailed payments as of the date received. If the payment is: (1) received by 5 p.m. local time at the address shown on the remittance slip on the front of your monthly statement; (2) paid with a check drawn in U.S. dollars on a U.S. financial institution or a U.S. dollar money order; and (3) sent in the return envelope with only the remittance portion of your statement accompanying it. Payments received by mail after 5 p.m. local time at the remittance address on any day including the Payment Due Date, but that otherwise meet the above requirements, will be credited as of the next day. Payments made online or by phone will be credited as of the date of receipt if made by 5 p.m. Central. Credit for any other payments may be delayed up to five days.

No payment shall operate as an accord and satisfaction without the prior written approval of one of our Senior Officers.

We process most payment checks electronically by using the information found on your check. Each check authorizes us to create a one-time electronic funds transfer (or process it as a check or paper draft). Funds may be withdrawn from your account as soon as the same day we receive your payment. Checks are not returned to you. For more information or to stop the electronic funds transfers, call us at the number listed on the front.

If you have authorized us to pay your credit card bill automatically from your savings or checking account with us, you can stop the payment on any amount you think is wrong. To stop payment, your letter must reach us at least three business days before the automatic payment is scheduled to occur.

## TOTAL INTEREST CHARGE COMPUTATION

Interest Charges accrue and are compounded on a daily basis. To determine the Interest Charges we multiply each Balance Subject to Interest Rate by its applicable Daily Periodic Rate and that result is multiplied by the number of days in the billing cycle. To determine the total Interest Charge for the billing cycle, we add the Periodic Rate Interest Charges together. A Daily Periodic Rate is calculated by dividing an Annual Percentage Rate by 365.

## HOW WE ALLOCATE YOUR PAYMENTS

Payments are allocated to posted balances. If your account has balances with different APRs, we will allocate the amount of your payment equal to the Total Minimum Payment Due to the lowest APR balances first (including transactions made after this statement). Payment amounts in excess of your Total Minimum Payment Due will be applied to balances with higher APRs before balances with lower APRs.

## IMPORTANT INFORMATION ABOUT PAYMENTS BY PHONE

When using the optional Pay-by-Phone service, you authorize us to initiate an electronic payment from your account at the financial institution you designate. You must authorize the amount and timing of each payment. For your protection, we will ask for security information. A fee may apply for expedited service. To cancel, call us before the scheduled payment date. Same-day payments cannot be edited or canceled.

## YOUR CREDIT LINES

The Total Credit Line is the amount of credit available for the account; however, only a portion of that is available for Bank Cash Advances. The Cash Credit Line is that amount you have available for Bank Cash Advances. Generally, Bank Cash Advances consist of ATM Cash Advances, Over the Counter (OTC) Cash Advances, Same-Day Online Cash Advances, Overdraft Protection Cash Advances, Cash Equivalents, and applicable transaction fees.

## MISCELLANEOUS

Virtual cards are the digital form of your eligible physical credit cards stored within a digital wallet.

For the complete terms and conditions of your account, consult your Credit Card Agreement. This account is issued and administered by FIA Card Services. FIA Card Services is a registered trademark of FIA Card Services and/or its affiliates.

**If your billing address or contact information has changed, or if your address is incorrect as it appears on this bill, please provide all corrections here.**

Address 1

Address 2

City

State _____ Zip

Area Code & Home Phone

Area Code & Work Phone

The daily balance is calculated every night and the finance charge is calculated daily. The sum of each of the daily calculations is then added for the entire month. You will note that when the total outstanding balance is low and the calculated finance charge for the period is less than $1 or $2, the bank is allowed to charge you a "Minimum Finance Charge" and that is applied instead of the smaller amount. This is allowed by law.

Remember, the finance charge is an interest charge for the money outstanding that you owe the bank. Since that amount you really owe them at any point in time is a combination of previous purchases less any payment or credits, that amount can be different every single day. As such, they are allowed to charge interest for the exact balance you owe on that day. Hence, the reason for the daily calculation.

In summary, the following points cannot be over emphasized:

- If you are stuck in a high credit card debt situation – do whatever you can to alleviate yourself from it. Curb your spending. Apply for or see if you can get a debt consolidation loan. Apply for or see if you can get a 0% for one-year balance transfer credit card to consolidate the debt and pay 0% interest for one year.
- Do what you can to pay all your credit card balances off every month completely. This is the optimal situation where you are getting the advantage of using the bank's money for free (and as a substitute for cash) and you are living within your means.
- You should never use credit cards to buy something now that you really cannot afford. If you can't afford it now – how do you expect to afford it later? And, for the convenience of getting it now, you have to pay a premium

(finance charges or interest) unless you pay it back in one month.

- Remember that a credit card is nothing more than a fancy way to say you are taking out an expensive short-term loan – because that is what it is. Unless you plan to pay it back in one month – it is probably not a good financially sound decision. There are exceptions, but you need to be smart on how you make those exception decisions to make sure you are doing what is best for you financially.

Finally, I cannot stress enough that it is never too late to correct your ways and use credit cards to your advantage. Credit Cards are an excellent way to boost your credit and make you an excellent consumer. But you need to control the credit card and not let it control you. If you feel like the credit card is controlling you – it is time to stop using them and get your financial house in order. Be wise and control your credit card debt. It will make you a much better financial consumer survivor.

# Chapter 9
# Loan Interest

When you use someone else's money (the bank, the loan company, whoever) to spend on something today, with the promise that you will pay them back in the future (weekly, monthly, whatever the payment cycle) that someone else is going to charge you to do that – since – you are spending their money NOW.  For the privilege of spending this money today, you have to pay a fee, or interest.

The reason you have to pay this fee is because money that is present money – here and now – is earned money, readily available to spend NOW.  Since the future is not guaranteed, your future payment money may not happen. Thus, the person fronting you the money now is taking a risk that you may not pay them back.  When someone takes a risk, they receive a reward, or fee for taking that risk.

To demonstrate this, let's take a simple example.  Just this week your clothes washing machine broke and the repair person told you that it is over 15 years old and very difficult to get repair parts.  Additionally, the total cost to repair it would probably not be worth it since, after it was fixed, you would still have a 15-year-old washer for the cost of what a new one would cost you today.  You see a nice washer that you would like to buy at the appliance store.  The dishwasher is $900.  But you don't have $900 in cash to pay for it right now.  You have several options:

1.  If you had enough money in your checking account and could afford it – you could use your debit card and pay for it right away
2.  You could ask your parents or another family member to give you the money now and you promise to pay them back later.
3.  You could pay for the washer with a credit card
4.  Finally, you could get some sort of short term loan or financing from the appliance store or a bank or some other short term lender

There are probably a few other scenarios, but let's just look at these. First, you always have the option to just say – I can't afford this right now and walk away. That could be the best alternative – if you really can't afford the item. But you still need to wash your clothes and the closet laundromat is about a mile away. You could ask your neighbor next door to use their washer until you get a new one – but you aren't that close to them – plus you don't want to schlep you dirty clothes to someone's house! So, the bottom line is you really need this new washer and you need to find a way to pay for it. And to add insult to injury, you do not have an extra $900 sitting around in your checking or savings account —so option one is not really a good alternative.

Option two looks good, but you really don't want to bother you parents or your siblings for a loan. While they might not charge you interest, how fair is it to them to use their hard earned money today for something you want or need – when they may have a similar want of need?

You look at option three and think – what is the credit card interest rate? Well, you already have $5,000 on that card and the interest rate is 14.9% and last month's finance charge alone was about $60.

Adding on another $900 would put you close to $6,000 and the finance charge would be close to $75. The minimum payment was $115, and would probably increase to $125 or more. So, you really don't like that option.

That only leaves us with option four. Option four is, in most cases, is not a good option because most times, short-term financing will be at a high interest rate (like 10-20%). But this week is your lucky week since the appliance store is giving a short-term, 6-month, same as cash, financing option. Buy the washer today, take up to 6-months to pay back the money, and they will charge you no interest. Getting future money for free – yippee! – just like when you were a child!!

So, we definitely want to look at option four. But here are some very important things you need to consider – VERY IMPORTANT:

- Remember – no one wants to give you future money for free. The catch here is they want to sell that washer. So, they are willing to forgo the interest to make the sale today.
- Second – you better have really good credit. They probably won't give you the deal if you have had credit issues in the past. Remember – they are forgoing the interest to sell the washer – but, they also are willing to take the risk on you if you have a good loan-repayment history. They are willing to take the chance that you will pay the money back. Unlike your family, who may or may not see you pay them back – they will hunt you down find you if you don't pay them back.
- Third – read that 6-months same as cash agreement VERY CAREFULLY. I will guarantee you that there is a clause that if you miss one payment – they not only can charge

you one-month interest – but they can go back and re-
charge for all the interest for the loaned money for the
entire loan period. That's the big catch. They are counting
on you to pay them back TIMELY. If you don't, they get
all the money just like if they gave you a full-loan. And the
rate they charge is significantly more than the rate a bank
might charge. So be very careful.

The moral to this story is this – Short-term finance charges are just
a fancy word for loan interest. Anytime you are taking short-term
financing or a short-term loan, you need to pay the lender a fee –
interest – for them allowing you to spend their money today with
the future hope that you will pay them back tomorrow.

So now let's calculate the interest. The two key components for
calculated interest are the interest rate and the time – (the amount
of time it takes to pay the total amount of money back to the
person lending you the money). Many times, we focus on the
interest rate, however, we should not lose sight of the fact of the
amount of time the loan is outstanding. While that rate may be
good – the time is where the lenders make their money.

For example – if I take a loan for 1 month at a rate of 12% per
annum, I don't pay 12% since that is the rate for the entire year.
The effective total amount of interest I would pay would be 12/12
or 1% of the loan. On the other hand, if I take a loan for 10 years
at a rate of 12% per annum, I could pay as much as 10 x 12 or
120% of the loan. This is where it's get tricky.

Here is a simple example: Remember when we talked about the
fact that future money is not worth as much as present money.
Well that is even more pronounced the further out that future
money is coming back to the lender. For example, you borrow

$50,000 today from me and promise to pay it back to me in 10 years. Why on earth would I do this if all I got back was $50,000? In ten years, all prices will probably rise and that $50,000 will be worth *significantly* less than it is today! So, if I am loaning you a lot of money for a long term – I need to get interest for the WHOLE term of the loan – not just for one year. If the interest I charge you is 5% -- that is 5% PER YEAR not 5% for the entire term (ten years). If you promise to pay it all back to me at the end of the ten years – you don't pay me 50,000 x 1.05 or $52,500. That would only be $2500 in interest and for over ten years that would only be $250 per year for the money I gave to you ($50,000). That would only be .5% or ½ of one percent interest for the entire length of the loan.

No -- What I would expect at the end of ten years would be $50,000 x.05 = $2,500 per year or $25,000. So, you would owe me a total of $75,000! Now you look at this and say – hey, I am paying you 50% interest since I only borrowed $50,000 but I end up paying you back a total of $75,000 ($25,000 in interest) which is 50% more than the total I originally loaned you. But what you failed to realize is that you had that money outstanding for ten years. 5% interest per annum x 10 years is 50% interest. And that is not that bad considering you had the money for ten years and most things double about every ten years. If I kept that money and was able to double in ten years, I would actually have had $100,000 instead of the $75,000 you are paying me back.

So, it is always important to remember the length of time of the loan as well as the interest rate quoted. Almost always interest rates are quoted in annual terms - usually x% annually or per annum (per year). If you have a loan for more than one year – remember that you need to pay interest for EACH and EVERY year unless you are quoted a rate for the entire time period of the loan.

To get a more pronounced look at this let's say you take out a 30-year mortgage for $160,000. The interest rate for the loan is 4% (per year). When the loan is amortized (I will cover this term and its significance more in the chapter on mortgages), the resulting payment is $763.86 for the next 30 years.

Doing the math, $763.86 x 12 month per year x 30 years = $274,989.60. Notice – the total amount of money you give back to the bank is $274.989.60 for a $160,000 loan. In simple terms, you will pay $114,989.60 in interest over the life of the loan, which, some may argue is 71.87% interest. BUT – since it is a 30-year loan if you divide that by 30 years, it is in effect only an average of about 2.4% per year. The reason it is less than the 4% is because a portion of your payment is paying principal and the rest of the payment is paying interest. So, the outstanding principal balance is going down a little each year (i.e., each year you are actually owing the lender less the total $160,000).

For purposes of this chapter here are the important concepts to remember:

- Interest on loans is almost always quoted in an "annum" (annual) basis.
- The total dollar value amount of interest you pay on a loan is always a product of how much the loan is, the interest rate – AND that total LENGTH of time you take to pay the loan back. If you pay all loans in one year – than this is a moot point. However, since most loans are more than one year – you need to pay interest for the entire time the loan

is outstanding which is always more than you think you would pay if you only took the loan for one year.

- Interest calculations are not complex – but people need to understand that the absolute dollar amount of interest you pay is always more when you take a loan for more than one year because you owe the lender the money for more than one year.

- Interest is charged to you because the lender is giving you real money today to spend for the promise that you will pay them back in the future. Because they are taking a risk that you may or may not pay the money back (the money is not a sure thing), they charge you for taking on this risk. The riskier you are them, the more they will charge. The less risky you are to them, the less they will charge (lower interest).

- 0% interest (same as cash) deals are a wonderful way to use the lender's money for no interest charge – but be VERY CAREFUL. If you miss one payment – they get payback for all that back interest plus more (penalties and a higher interest rate). So, if you take advantage of these deals – make sure you have enough money to pay it back TIMELY – because if you don't, that wonderful deal you took will cost you plenty and a lot more than had you just taken a simple loan.

- Interest is always paid for loans because – as stated in chapter one – future money is worth LESS than present money you have today. So, for that privilege to use someone else's present money – you need to pay a fee to make up for the fact that the money you pay them back is worth less than what they borrowed you in the beginning.

*Ken Pyzik*

# Chapter 10
# Understanding Car Loans

Before you read this chapter, you need to understand that the goal of the car finance person is to get you to sign on for as much financing (read that to be loaned money) as possible. Their most important goal is to make money for the dealership – and the way they make money is selling financing (loaned money). Plain and simple – the more loaned money the better. Loaned money means interest which means profit for the dealership and commission for the finance guy. It's that simple. With that in mind, let's look at some of the facts surrounding car financing and car loans.

If you have gone to buy a car lately, you probably know the drill you go through. You see a car you like; you may test drive it and then you begin to negotiate with the salesman about how much you want to buy the car for. Negotiating is simply a part of the whole deal. It's not like buying a washing machine or a toaster. You see one you like, the price is X, you place it in your cart – and pay X and away you go. For some reason, cars are different. The price you see on the sticker (for new cars) is NOT the price you pay. That is the MSRP (manufacturers suggest retail price). A price that the manufacturer believes the car should sell for. Well, what is that price? In reality, that is a starting point for which you now can start to negotiate with the salesman what you are really going to pay.

The dealership has a lot of inventory or cars. Unlike the local consumer goods retailer (who purchases all the products and marks up the price to then sell them to you), the dealership has not really "purchased" all those vehicles to sell to you. He has taken out a line of credit with a local bank or with the manufacturer of the vehicles to sell them. So, there is no hard and fast price they need to sell the car for. Believe me – they will only negotiate so far – and they know where that magic number is. But without going into too much detail, let's just say that the price you pay for the vehicle is somewhere in the neighborhood of 90-95% of what the MSRP is.

So, once you have agreed upon a price – you sign the paper and go – right? Well, not exactly. This is where you go and sit and wait to see the car finance guy. His/her goal is to do one thing – get you to buy more extras and finance any and everything they can.

You see you went in the dealership to purchase a car – but what they are really selling is add-ons, extras, options, services, car warranties (which is nothing more than an insurance product), car matts, tinted windows, a seat for grandma, and so on and so on. Bet you did not know that, at the beginning of the day, you were not only going to purchase a vehicle – you were going to purchase many other products, services and insurance policies!

Anyway, almost all consumers will finance this purchase (i.e., take out a loan). The loan should be for just the vehicle, but the car finance guy will attempt to tack on all the extras, options, services and car warranties (because the dealership make a markup profit on those items) and get you to add those to the loan so that you are PAYING INTEREST on all sorts of things in addition to the vehicle. For example – you want tinted windows - that costs $300.

Place it on the loan – it's only an additional $8 a month on the loan. With the interest – you end up paying $350 for that product. You may get an excellent rate for your vehicle. But remember, if you want extras, pay for those separately and for cash if you can – don't include those in the loan – unless you don't mind paying interest for financing them.

So, let's look at the actual car loan. I have developed a spreadsheet that I think really helps when you go to purchase a vehicle. The things to remember are these:

- The thrill of buying a new vehicle can cloud your logical thinking. Remember, try to limit the additional options – particularly if you plan on financing. Sometimes it is best to pay for the options in cash
- If you have a budget amount that you want to stick to – be firm. The dealership wants to sell you a car – any car. Don't let them push you into something that is beyond your budget – no matter how much they try to impress you.
- Make sure to ask about dealer discounts – and use a spreadsheet to make sure they are counted in your deal. Many times, dealers will hoodwink uninformed consumers and leave the dealer and manufacturer discounts out. When dealer discounts are not taken – that is taken right back into the dealership as profit.

| Model Choice: | Car A You Want | |
|---|---|---|
| **Initial Price:** | $18,500.00 | |
| -------------------------------------------- | | |
| | | |
| Initial Price . . . . . . . . . . . | $18,500.00 | |
| Options Package(s). . . . . . . | 575.00 | |
| Total Vehicle Price . . . . . . . . . . . . | | $19,075.00 |
| | | |
| Dealer Discounts . . . . . . . . . | ($1,000.00) | |
| Est. Trade-In Allowance . . . . . . | (2,000.00) | |
| Total Payments/Allowance. . . . . . | | (3,000.00) |
| Subtotal before Tax and Down Payment. . . . | | $16,075.00 |
| | | |
| Documentation Fee . . . . . . . . . | 75.00 | |
| Sales Tax (6.75%) . . . . . . . . . . . | $1,090.13 | |
| License Transfer Fee . . . . . . . | 75.00 | |
| Total Tax and Other Fees . . . . . | | 1,240.13 |
| Subtotal before Down Payment. . . . . . . | | $17,315.13 |
| | | |
| Down Payment . . . . . . . . . . | | (4,000.00) |
| Net Finance Amount. . . . . . . . . . . . | | $13,315.13 |
| | | |
| Annual % Rate for Financing . . . . | 3.90% | |
| Number of Payments (Months) . . . . | 48 | |
| Total Interest Charges. . . . . . . | $1,087.15 | |
| Estimated Monthly Payments . . . . . . . . | | $300.05 |

- Finally, get any deal in writing – and make sure you know exactly where all the figures are coming from.  Many, many times – numbers are flying around and there are too many different combinations of numbers to remember them all.  Write down all the numbers – place them into a spreadsheet similar to what I have presented here – and work with numbers until you are happy with the deal.

Notice that I have tried to show that you should minimize the additional options that you get since, those will be included in the financing. I have also calculated what the payment will be and total interest you will pay over the life of the loan. The calculation for figuring out the loan payment is complex. Although I will show it here, I won't explain it in detail:

Financed Amount * ((Annual Interest Rate/12)/ (1-(1/((1+(Annual Interest Rate/12))^Number of Months of Financing))))

The calculation for the total interest throughout the life of the loan is simple. Take the payment amount times the number of payments, then subtract the amount financed from that total. Of course, if you are one of the lucky people that can get those 0% interest deals – jump on it if you can afford to since it will save you thousands in interest costs.

The purpose of showing this is to give you a tool to help you get the payment or deal that you can afford. If, after negotiating the deal, the dealership completes the paperwork and something is amiss – do not be timid and let them get away with it. Even if they say it is too much work to redo the paperwork – show them what you had in writing from them and make the numbers work out the way you think they should.

For example, perhaps this has happened to you. You go to the dealership, negotiate a deal, finally decide on options and financing and you get ready to sign the papers. Suddenly, when you go to sign, it appears that the numbers are all different. The dealer says that there was a destination charge – or this and that miscellaneous fee and now it appears that the total is about $800 to $1000 more than you expected. What just happened? You had a deal at price X and the final price is X + $1000?

This is why you want to place as much in writing BEFORE you sign the real paperwork. Once you sign the paperwork – that is the final deal. Also, make sure to tell the salesman the number you want INCLUDING all fees, taxes, extras, etc. If you truly want some extra options, go ahead and pay for those separately (if you can afford to), but stick to your budget and make sure you get a read on all the extra fees, taxes, etc., before you sign the paper and see a much larger number than you anticipated.

Finally, remember, car loans are not that complicated. What makes them complex is that when you boil it all down, most car loans (especially new cars) are not just a loan for the vehicle alone. Almost always it is financing for purchasing a basket of goodies which happens to include the car! My advice – if you want to purchase a new car is to purchase the car – not all the other stuff. Finance the car – not all the other stuff. Make sure you know all the fees you need to pay upfront –so that you can effectively plan for the purchase and stay within your budget. Too many times people end up purchasing a brand new car – and while they are happy with the vehicle, they ended up breaking their budget because of all the extra goodies that were tacked onto the deal.

# Chapter 11
# Mortgages and Mortgage Payments

Probably the largest consumer finance item that impacts many people is a mortgage. Mortgages are loans that are taken to purchase a home. If you pay rent for an apartment to live in, a mortgage is the same type of payment with some very important differences. When paying rent – you are paying for the privilege to live in someone else's home or apartment (i.e., they own the property). When you take out a mortgage, you are paying back a loan that you took out to pay for the property that you now "own" (I say that – but you technically don't own it – the bank or group that holds the loan note owns the property). In other words, with renting, you own no property – with a mortgage you own the property once the mortgage is paid off.

Obtaining a mortgage loan is not an easy task for someone who is trying to get a mortgage for the first time. There is a combination of several factors that affect whether you will get approved for a mortgage loan. Here is a list of most of those factors:
- Your credit worthiness (as assessment of how well the lender thinks you can pay the loan back); this is based upon many factors – but primarily your current credit score
- Affordability of the mortgage, which includes - income to debt ratio, and your ability to demonstrate that you can pay the loan back.

- The amount of the loan and the amount of the down payment
- The appraised value of the property
- The type of mortgage loan you are undertaking

Other factors may also include the type of property you are buying, the area where are you buying it, etc. The most important factors are the ones a consumer can control – namely, your credit worthiness and the affordability (what you can really afford). On the first factor, you can control your credit worthiness by making sure you pay your bills on time, not getting into too much debt and following some of the advice I have outlined in this book. On the second factor, affordability, there are a wide difference in views as to what someone can properly afford.

MortgageCalculator.org does a marvelous job of explaining everything about mortgages. It has a wonderful quote on affordability:

*"The old formula that was used to determine how much a borrower could afford was about three times the gross annual income. However, this formula has proven to not always be reliable. It is safer and more realistic to look at the individual budget and figure out how much money there is to spare and what the monthly payments on a new house will be. When figuring out what kind of mortgage payment one can afford, other factors such as taxes maintenance, insurance, and other expenses should be factored. Usually, lenders want borrowers having monthly payments exceeding more than 28% to 44% of the borrower's monthly income. For those who have excellent credit, the lender may allow the payments to exceed 44%. To aid in this determination, banks and websites like this one offer mortgage calculators to assist in determining the mortgage payment that one can afford."*

Interesting isn't!  Notice that the number one way to assist in figuring out affordability is to look at the individual budget - as we do in chapter 4.

MortgageCalculator.org also has some other very good tips, information, calculators, advice, and a great glossary that I believe everyone should read before their first time going in to get a mortgage.

So, let's focus on mortgage affordability and how to calculate your mortgage payment since these are the two most important things you should consider before signing the dotted line for a mortgage.

Mortgage affordability is a very individualized process.  Similarly, to household budgeting, deciding upon how much of a mortgage payment you can afford really depends upon your lifestyle, spending habits, ability to budget, discipline and ability to truly understand where all your income and expenses are being allocated.  Mortgage affordability is plainly about making sure that you are practicing effective budgeting

This may seem simplistic – but it is reality.  Too many times people take on an adjustable rate mortgage because it has a payment they can afford today.  But when the rate changes or the mortgage payment increases, it simply "breaks" their budget.  So, let's explore how to really find a mortgage payment that you can afford.

On the next page, I have included a sample budget document where the person is paying $800 for a condo. Their real estate taxes and condo insurance are shown separately although many times these are included in the mortgage payment – unless you specifically ask them not to be. This is an important concept you need to take into consideration.

20XX Personal Budget

| | | Jan | Feb | Mar | Apr | May | Jun | Jul | Aug | Sep | Oct | Nov | Dec | Totals | % |
|---|---|---|---|---|---|---|---|---|---|---|---|---|---|---|---|
| | 1 | | | | | | | | | | | | | 0.00 | |
| | 2 | | | | | | | | | | | | | 0.00 | |
| VISA/CC | 3 | 50.00 | 50.00 | 50.00 | 50.00 | 50.00 | 50.00 | 50.00 | 50.00 | 50.00 | 50.00 | 50.00 | 50.00 | 600.00 | 2.35% |
| Other Debt payments | 4 | 175.00 | 175.00 | 175.00 | 175.00 | 175.00 | 175.00 | 175.00 | 175.00 | 175.00 | 175.00 | 175.00 | 175.00 | 2100.00 | 8.22% |
| Savings | 5 | 150.00 | 150.00 | 150.00 | 150.00 | 150.00 | 150.00 | 150.00 | 150.00 | 150.00 | 150.00 | 150.00 | 150.00 | 1800.00 | 7.04% |
| | 6 | | | | | | | | | | | | | 0.00 | 0.00% |
| Internet/TV Service | 7 | 101.75 | 101.75 | 101.75 | 101.75 | 101.75 | 101.75 | 101.75 | 101.75 | 101.75 | 101.75 | 101.75 | 101.75 | 1221.00 | 4.78% |
| | 8 | | | | | | | | | | | | | 0.00 | 0.00% |
| Cell Phone service | 9 | 52.34 | 52.34 | 52.34 | 52.34 | 52.34 | 52.34 | 52.34 | 52.34 | 52.34 | 52.34 | 52.34 | 52.34 | 628.08 | 2.46% |
| Car/Truck Plates | 10 | | | | | 78.00 | | | | | | | | 78.00 | 0.31% |
| Power (Electric) | 11 | 45.00 | 45.00 | 45.00 | 45.00 | 45.00 | 45.00 | 45.00 | 45.00 | 45.00 | 45.00 | 45.00 | 45.00 | 540.00 | 2.11% |
| | 12 | | | | | | | | | | | | | 0.00 | 0.00% |
| | 13 | | | | | | | | | | | | | 0.00 | 0.00% |
| | 14 | | | | | | | | | | | | | 0.00 | 0.00% |
| Life Ins | 15 | | | | | 278.00 | | | | | | | | 278.00 | 1.09% |
| Condo Ins. | 16 | | 335.00 | | | | | | | | | | | 335.00 | 1.31% |
| | 17 | | | | | | | | | | | | | 0.00 | 0.00% |
| | 18 | | | | | | | | | | | | | 0.00 | 0.00% |
| Gas Bill | 19 | 20.00 | 20.00 | 20.00 | 20.00 | 20.00 | 20.00 | 20.00 | 20.00 | 20.00 | 20.00 | 20.00 | 20.00 | 240.00 | 0.94% |
| | 20 | | | | | | | | | | | | | 0.00 | 0.00% |
| | 21 | | | | | | | | | | | | | 0.00 | 0.00% |
| Car Payment | 22 | 250.00 | 250.00 | 250.00 | 250.00 | 250.00 | 250.00 | 250.00 | 250.00 | 250.00 | 250.00 | 250.00 | 250.00 | 3000.00 | 11.74% |
| Car Ins | 23 | 75.00 | 75.00 | 75.00 | 75.00 | 75.00 | 75.00 | 75.00 | 75.00 | 75.00 | 75.00 | 75.00 | 75.00 | 900.00 | 3.52% |
| Oil/Gas/Maint for Car | 24 | 72.73 | 65.23 | 60.00 | 78.50 | 89.53 | 75.00 | 75.00 | 75.00 | 75.00 | 75.00 | 75.00 | 75.00 | 890.99 | 3.49% |
| | 25 | | | | | | | | | | | | | 0.00 | 0.00% |
| Unexpected Expense | 26 | | 212.30 | | 73.00 | | | | | | | | | 285.30 | 1.12% |
| | 27 | | | | | | | | | | | | | 0.00 | 0.00% |
| | 28 | | | | | | | | | | | | | 0.00 | 0.00% |
| | 29 | | | | | | | | | | | | | 0.00 | 0.00% |
| | 30 | | | | | | | | | | | | | 0.00 | 0.00% |
| Misc Cash Expense | 31 | 120.00 | 120.00 | 60.00 | 80.00 | 80.00 | 80.00 | 80.00 | 80.00 | 80.00 | 80.00 | 80.00 | 80.00 | 1020.00 | 3.99% |
| Entertainment/Vacation | | | | | | | | | | | | | | 0.00 | 0.00% |
| Total Budget Items | | 1111.82 | 1651.62 | 1039.09 | 1150.59 | 1166.62 | 1352.09 | 1074.09 | 1074.09 | 1074.09 | 1074.09 | 1074.09 | 1074.09 | 13916.37 | 54.45% |
| | | | | | | | | | | | | | | 0.00 | |
| Quarterly/Monthly Assess | | 45.00 | 45.00 | 45.00 | 45.00 | 45.00 | 45.00 | 45.00 | 45.00 | 45.00 | 45.00 | 45.00 | 45.00 | 540.00 | 2.11% |
| REAL ESTATE Taxes | | 375.87 | | | 375.87 | | | 375.87 | | | 375.87 | | | 1503.48 | 5.88% |
| Mortgage/Rent | | 800.00 | 800.00 | 800.00 | 800.00 | 800.00 | 800.00 | 800.00 | 800.00 | 800.00 | 800.00 | 800.00 | 800.00 | 9600.00 | 37.56% |
| TOTAL CASH OUTFLOW | | 2332.69 | 2496.62 | 1884.09 | 2371.46 | 2011.62 | 2197.09 | 2294.96 | 1919.09 | 1919.09 | 2294.96 | 1919.09 | 1919.09 | 25559.85 | 100.00% |
| CASH INFLOWS | | | | | | | | | | | | | | | |
| Interest | | | | | | | | | | | | | | 0.00 | |
| Pensions/Ret.Inc/other | | | | | | | | | | | | | | 0.00 | |
| Work Check 1 | | 1328.73 | 1328.73 | 1328.73 | 1328.73 | 1328.73 | 1328.73 | 1328.73 | 1328.73 | 1328.73 | 1328.73 | 1328.73 | 1328.73 | 15944.76 | |
| Work Check 2 | | 1328.73 | 1328.73 | 1328.73 | 1328.73 | 1328.73 | 1328.73 | 1328.73 | 1328.73 | 1328.73 | 1328.73 | 1328.73 | 1328.73 | 15944.76 | |
| Deposits | | | | | | | | | | | | | | 0.00 | |
| TOTAL CASH INFLOW | | 2657.46 | 2657.46 | 2657.46 | 2657.46 | 2657.46 | 2657.46 | 2657.46 | 2657.46 | 2657.46 | 2657.46 | 2657.46 | 2657.46 | 31889.52 | |
| NET CASH FLOW | | 324.77 | 160.84 | 773.37 | 286.00 | 645.84 | 460.37 | 362.50 | 738.37 | 738.37 | 362.50 | 738.37 | 738.37 | 6329.67 | |

Most mortgage companies will not allow you to have a mortgage unless you include the insurance and taxes with the payment. They call this escrow. I dislike escrow – but most people either are forced by banks to do it – or just don't know any better and just do it.

To them, it is just fine that the bank includes the taxes and insurance with their monthly mortgage payment. The bank likes it because, they can ask for 2 or 3 months of advance taxes and insurances when you close. This is a significant expense and, it gives the bank 3 months of free money for which they do not have to pay any interest. Multiply that by many mortgages and it's a lot of extra money. Plus, it assures them that you have insurance if something should happen to the house and you refuse to pay the money back. If possible, I always try to exclude the taxes and insurance from the mortgage payment and I like to budget those items and pay for them myself. Many individuals will not be so lucky – so just make sure you discuss this with the banker/lender of the mortgage to find out if you can do this or if they won't allow it.

At any rate – for this example, we assume that you do not have to pay escrow and that can control your own real estate taxes and insurance on the property and we show then as separate expenses of the sheet. So, you have decided that you want to purchase a new property. You already know that you can at least afford what you are already paying – $800 a month as well as the taxes and insurance

Currently you have $6300 of "extra" income in your budget (that you are hopefully saving) and the $1500 currently going for real estate taxes, which will go to pay for real estate taxes on the new

house. Either way, we have $800 per month going for rent and
$6300 yearly excess. So, you can probably afford to purchase a
new home. But how much of a home can you afford? Therein lies
the huge question that you could get 10 different answers for!
Here is how I would look at it:

Affordability Answer – My belief is that you should never
purchase a house where the payment would be more than 33% of
your annual income (TAKE HOME PAY). Some financial
analysts and gurus will say you can go as high as 40% - but I think
33% should be your maximum.

So, if we take the annual income ($31,889) x 33% = $10,523 –
then divide that by 12, you get $876.95 (not including taxes and
insurance). Since you are currently paying $800 per month, you
are in a good situation. But now how much of a house can you
purchase if you do not want the maximum payment to be more
than the $877? Well there are several mortgage calculators that
can do this – but basically you should know that it is a product of
the following factors:
- The interest rate you will pay
- The number of years you take out the loan
- The amount of down payment you will give when you go
  to purchase the house (the remainder being the loaned
  amount)

These three factors can vary, and based upon how you vary them –
it will give you a good range of the house you can buy. So, let's
assume you can get 4% interest on a standard 30-year fixed rate
loan and that you plan to put down 20% as a down payment. If
you plug in the numbers into a mortgage calculator you will get to
around $230,000 with a $46,000 down payment, which means you

are financing $184,000 and at 4% for a standard 30-year mortgage the payment would be $878.44.

So, based upon this affordability index (33% of take home pay), you could afford a $230,000 home. But before I go on to the next affordability calculation, be aware that this takes all of the excess money you have in excess of your budget ($6300) and that it assumes you will be paying the taxes and insurance yourself (no escrow). If you have to take escrow, the payment would be larger, but those items in your current budget would cover it. Additionally, since you are putting down 20% you will probably not have to get PMI (private mortgage insurance).

For just a moment, I would like to talk about PMI. PMI is protection for the bank when you are unable to pay your loan. Many people strapped for cash, will put only 5 or 10% down on a home thinking this is a good way to get a home when they do not have enough for a down payment. For the bank to take on this additional risk, they charge you PMI – the premium costs to take out a private mortgage insurance policy in case you default on the loan. The bank or lender see you only placing 5 or 10% down as a risky venture. It is easier for you to walk away from a loan where you only place 5 or 10% as opposed to placing 20% or more. In our case, a 5% down payment on $230,000 is only $11,500 as opposed to $46,000 which is 20%. Think about this from the bank's perspective – how much easier is it for you to walk away from a loan where you only invested $11,500 as opposed to investing $46,000.

PMI gives the lender piece of mind that if you walk away, they have something to collect on. It gives you nothing but an additional cost to your mortgage. Therefore, before we go onto the next affordability index remember this – if you cannot come up with at least 20% down payment to purchase home – I recommend that you NOT purchase the home because the additional PMI cost is wasted money – a wasted expense that you do not want to have. Many people will scoff at this and say, "well if that is the case – many people will never buy a home", and I understand that. However, paying PMI should be a last resort. Try to avoid getting it on your loan.

Let's look at another affordability calculation for purchasing a home. I have seen many people purchase homes that they really could not afford mainly because they did not anticipate all the additional costs involved with purchasing a home. When you try to scrape together a down payment – having any money left over is tough. So, if you buy a home where you are really stretching the limits and then something unexpected happens like something for the kids, something with the car, or you need a sudden repair (like a furnace or air conditioner replacement) you can be in a world of hurt. Unfortunately, if you worry too much about these things, you will never purchase a home!

So, on the next page is a table that shows an affordability calculation that is more practical (using the numbers from the budget in this chapter and chapter 4):

## Realistic Home Affordability Calculation

| | | |
|---|---|---|
| Annual Income (Take home pay) | $ 31,889.00 | |
| Multiply by 40% | | $ 12,755.60 |
| Subtract - Home Contingency Fund | | $ (1,200.00) |
| Subtract - Additional Monthly Utility Bill increase (5%) | | $ (200.00) |
| Add raise | | $ 360.00 |
| Add one month no rent | | $ 800.00 |
| Subtract yearly taxes | | $ (1,508.00) |
| Subtract yearly insurance | | $ (335.00) |
| | | |
| Sum of available income for payments | | $ 10,672.60 |
| Divide by 12 | | $ 889.38 |

This affordability calculation takes into account a "home contingency fund", which is above and beyond regular savings. This fund is there in case when you move into the house and a pipe breaks, or the air conditioner goes out, or an appliance breaks, etc. Many people don't realize that when you rent, if something goes wrong, the landlord fixes it. But once you own the home, you are responsible. Also, many people do not purchase a brand new home. So, this contingency is also there in case you want to re-paint a room or change the carpeting for a new wood floor, etc.

I would also like to point out that normally you will be going into a bigger living space than where you are now. This usually means that there will be an increase of at least 5% on the utility costs – water, gas, electric, cable /internet.

There is also one additional benefit that will occur when you move into your new home. You will probably have the luxury of not paying your first payment for at least one month. While this may seem illogical, due to the way the lenders structure the mortgages, your first payment will usually not be due until about 6 weeks from when you close – which means you may have one or two months with no payments!  It really isn't free – believe me, you are paying interest on the money you are lending from the first day you are taking it. However, depending upon on how the close is structured, you will have a month or two with no payment.

As you review this list, you will see that I have added a few more items and then I divided by 12 to see what monthly payment I could really afford. As you will note, it is still pretty close to the 33% that I feel you should be at, but it does not necessarily mean it will be. Each situation will be different, and, it is up to you to be realistic in your calculation.

The moral of this second calculation is to try to plan for some contingencies and don't forget to be realistic about what your true new costs will be to make sure you are purchasing something that you really can afford.

It is also important to understand how mortgage payments are calculated, what they mean, what is amortization, and why this all appears so complicated.

When you take out a mortgage, you are borrowing a lot of someone else's money (the bank or an investor). You pay them back in payments and, those payments include a portion of principal, (the actual amount you owe) and interest (the fee you must pay to use someone else's money today for the promise that you will pay them back).  Remember the three important concepts about "future money" and "payments" from Chapter 1:

1.  Present money is ALWAYS worth more than future money.  Money I have in my hands right now is worth more than a future promise of money.  The reason: Money I have now is worth what it is worth RIGHT NOW – future money is basically worth less because it is NOT, and never can be, 100% guaranteed.

2.  For the privilege to spend somebody else's present money with a payment of your future money, it costs you interest or a fee or some other cost above and beyond your future money since, (see #1), future money is worth less than present money.

3.  While we never pay interest or fees when we are kids, in the real world no one is going to give you present money to spend today for the cost of just your future promise of money in the future.  (There are rare exceptions to this with cars being sold for 0% financing – but take my word for it, if you miss one payment – it is no longer free).

Well, mortgages are the granddaddy of this process.  Since you are borrowing a lot of money for 15 or 30 years, you bet the bank or lender wanted to make sure they get their interest – from DAY 1! And the way you calculate the payment and interest is through a calculation called amortization.  Amortization has several meanings – but for purposes of this book – I like one of the definitions I saw from Wikipedia:

*"When used in the context of a home purchase, amortization is the process by which loan principal decreases over the life of a loan*

*.... (When a) mortgage payment is made, a portion of the payment is applied towards reducing the principal, and another portion of the payment is applied towards paying the interest on the loan. An amortization schedule, a table detailing each periodic payment on a loan, shows this ratio of principal and interest and demonstrates how a loan's principal amount decreases over time."*

The mathematical formula used to calculate this is as follows:

$$A = P \frac{r\left(1+r\right)^n}{\left(1+r\right)^n - 1}$$

where:

$A$ = payment Amount (per payment period, in this case monthly)
$P$ = initial Principal (loan amount)
$r$ = interest rate per period
$n$ = total number of payments or periods

Which, through a series of manipulations can be changed to be: $A = P*(r/(1-(1/((1+r)^n))))$, which allows you to place this formula in Excel.

Although this may seem very complicated, if you study the definition, the formula is calculating the amount of interest and the amount or principal reduction in the loan that is occurring over time. To understand this a little more clearly, I developed a spreadsheet that demonstrates how this works.

## Mortgage Amortization

| | | | | | |
|---|---|---|---|---|---|
| **Enter the Mortgage Amount =>** | | **$160,000** | | | |
| **Enter Interest Rate  ======>** | | **4.00** | **Effective Rate (monthly)** | | **0.33%** |
| **Enter the Number of Years =>** | | **15** | **Total No. of Payments** | | **180** |
| **Monthly Payment will be =>** | | **$1,183.50** | | | |
| **If an extra amount will be added** | | | **Loan Points/Fees** | | |
| **to principal, enter it here ===>** | | **$0.00** | **Amt. Deductible per year** | | |

| Payment No. | Date | Principal | Interest | Extra on Principal | Outstanding Balance |
|---|---|---|---|---|---|
| 1 | Sep-12 | $650.17 | $533.33 | $0.00 | $159,349.83 |
| 2 | Oct-12 | $652.33 | $531.17 | $0.00 | $158,697.50 |
| 3 | Nov-12 | $654.51 | $528.99 | $0.00 | $158,042.99 |
| 4 | Dec-12 | $656.69 | $526.81 | $0.00 | $157,386.30 |
| 5 | Jan-13 | $658.88 | $524.62 | $0.00 | $156,727.42 |
| 6 | Feb-13 | $661.08 | $522.42 | $0.00 | $156,066.34 |
| 7 | Mar-13 | $663.28 | $520.22 | $0.00 | $155,403.06 |
| 8 | Apr-13 | $665.49 | $518.01 | $0.00 | $154,737.57 |
| 9 | May-13 | $667.71 | $515.79 | $0.00 | $154,069.86 |
| 10 | Jun-13 | $669.93 | $513.57 | $0.00 | $153,399.93 |
| 11 | Jul-13 | $672.17 | $511.33 | $0.00 | $152,727.76 |
| 12 | Aug-13 | $674.41 | $509.09 | $0.00 | $152,053.35 |

Amortization schedules are available from several different websites on the net. However, this spreadsheet allows you to easily see what effect adding additional principal payments will make to shortening the life of the loan.

Here are a few things to note about the spreadsheet.

1. Remembering that you always have to pay interest on the outstanding balance, the calculation for the interest is simply the previous month's outstanding balance multiplied by the effectively monthly interest rate (which is the annual rate divided by 12).

2. Once you know how much interest you have to pay, subtract that from the monthly payment amount and you have the amount of principal you are paying as part of the payment.

3. At any time, if you want to increase the payment, you can apply that to the "Extra on Principal".

4. The Outstanding principal balance is calculated by taking the previous outstanding principal, subtract the amount of principal you are paying this month and then subtract any additional principal you paid and you get the "new" outstanding principal (the amount of money you still really own the lender).

What is nice about using this spreadsheet is that you can see and control the amount of outstanding principal you owe on the loan at any point in time. This is the amount you really owe on the loan.

It is also interesting to note, that, over the entire life of the loan, you will pay more than 1.5 or 2 times amount of interest compared to the original amount you borrowed. While this may not seem intuitive to you – this spreadsheet demonstrates the reason why this happens.  Because – you are paying interest on the amount of outstanding borrowed money over the entire life of the loan.  If you were to ask me for a simple 5% loan on $100,000 and said you would pay the loan off in one year and I only asked for one lump sum payment at the end of the loan, you would pay me back $105,000.  If you asked for one lump sum payment after 30 years – you would have to pay me back $5,000 for each year (in this case 30 x 5 or $150,000).  Now you might thing that is 1.5 times the original loan – but it is not!  You are paying me interest at 5% PER YEAR – for each year you have the money loaned to you.  This is why the interest amount seems high.  It really is not.  Interest rates are usually quoted in ANNUAL terms – the percentage of interest on the loan principal balance owed PER YEAR.   This also demonstrates the most important time element of interest.  If you paid me only $105,000 after 30 years, I would lose the opportunity to take the $100,000 and make 5% PER year.

That is why it is very important to understand how long you take a loan out. Whether it be a mortgage, car loan or any loan, you can always lower the payments if you take more time to pay.  BUT – and this is key -- if you take longer to pay off a loan, any loan – you will pay more real interest on that loan because you will be paying for the privilege of having the money lent to you for a longer period of time.

This is a nice segue to the final topic on mortgages – mortgage product variations and the pros and cons of each.  There are hundreds of books and advisor articles about mortgages and how to use them or how to pay them down, etc.  My purpose is to discuss different mortgage products and how you can select the best product for your personal situation.

I have categorized the most prevalent mortgage products that are available to the average consumer (from an interest rate perspective):

1. Fixed Rate Mortgage
   - 15-year
   - 30-year

2. Adjustable Rate Mortgage

3. Balloon Mortgage
   - Interest Only Mortgage

Fixed rate mortgages are normal mortgage that most people get. They are called fixed rate since they follow the standard amortization calculation that I showed earlier in the chapter and the interest rate is fixed throughout the whole term of the loan. They usually come in two flavors – the 15-year and the 30-year, which is to say the amount of time you plan to pay the borrowed money back to the lender. In the past few years 20-year, 10-year and even 40-year products have shown up.

The fixed rate mortgage allows you to always know what your payment will be. In addition, if you do not escrow with the lender (i.e., you pay your own insurance and real estate taxes), and if you have no PMI (private mortgage insurance), with a fixed rate mortgage your payment will be exactly the same for the life of the loan. This is ideal because it gives you the most control over being able to budget to pay the mortgage back.

In addition to the payment consistency, the fixed rate mortgage gives you the knowledge of locking in the interest rate for the loan duration so you never have to worry about paying a higher payment later in the life of the loan (e.g., in 5 years) if the interest rates increase.  For this reason, the interest rates are always a little higher when you get these since the bank is locking in that rate for the whole time period.   For example, if you get a 30-year mortgage at 4% today and interest rates skyrocket to 10% a year from now, you will still only pay 4% and you will pay 4% for as long as you have the mortgage.  Conversely, years ago when interest rates were high, if you had a fixed rate mortgage at let's say 13%, and interest rates zoomed down to 4%, you will still be stuck paying 13% unless you re-financed.  (Re-financing is a topic I would love to address, but it is a more advanced topic that you should research on your own.  When you fell you understand the concepts presented in this book, you will be ready to determine if a refinance is beneficial to you).

The only disadvantage of a fixed rate loan is if interest rates go down.  But you can always re-finance (get a new mortgage at a lower interest).

If you can afford it, always try to get a 15-year mortgage instead of the 30-year.  The 15-year mortgage means you have to pay the mortgage back in half the time of the 30-year mortgage – but you should note that the payment is NOT double.  In other words, for a $160,000 mortgage at 4% for a 30-year term, the payment is $763.86.  For the exact same mortgage at 4% for a 15-year term, the payment is $1183.50 or about a little more than 1 ½ times – not 2x.  So instead of paying double the money in half the time – you are paying 1 ½ times the money in half the time.

You may ask why this is?  Here is the reason – it all has to do with the interest.  Since you have the money out for 15 more years, you have to pay for 15 years more interest.  And the rate at which the interest decreases is not as quickly as the 15 year, therefore, you end up paying more interest over the time period for the first 15 years than you would if you have just taken a 15-year mortgage. In fact, if you look at an amortization schedule and look at a 30-year mortgage, after the first 15 years' worth of payments you would still owe more than 64% of the loan (see the number below from the table of a $160,000 loan at 4% for 30 years as opposed to 15:

| 179 | Oct-27 | $416.85 | $347.01 | $0.00 | $103,686.72 |
|-----|--------|---------|---------|-------|-------------|
| 180 | Nov-27 | $418.24 | $345.62 | $0.00 | $103,268.48 |
| 181 | Dec-27 | $419.64 | $344.23 | $0.00 | $102,848.84 |

Take the exact same loan at 15 years and at the 180th payment looks like this:

| 179 | Oct-27 | $1,175.65 | $7.85 | $0.00 | $1,179.57 |
|-----|--------|-----------|-------|-------|-----------|
| 180 | Nov-27 | $1,179.57 | $3.93 | $0.00 | $0.00 |

So, with a 30-year mortgage, even after 15 years, you still owe more than 64% of the loan. Of course, many people cannot afford the payment of a 15-year mortgage – but if you can – it is definitely in your advantage – particularly if you plan to keep the loan for the entire mortgage period.

Another type pf mortgage is the adjustable rate mortgage. The adjustable rate mortgage came out about 20 or 25 year ago when interest rates were high. Big banks and lenders had 3% and 4% loans on their books – but interest rates were in the teens. No one was getting a mortgage since interest rates were high and, those who had a mortgage were perfectly fine paying 3% or 4% instead of 13% or 14% for a new refinanced mortgage. The banks were not making enough money and no one was purchasing homes or refinancing. So, in order to get people to borrow money again to pay for houses, banks would entice borrowers with a lower interest rate that would stay constant for 3 or 5 or 7 years – but then would adjust to the rates at the time. In other words, if rates went up, the banks could re-coup some of that additional interest potential, and if rates went down, consumers could actually get a decrease in the rate on their loan. Sounds a good idea, right? Well not exactly.

Adjustable rate mortgages fueled an unfortunate situation where consumers got in with a lower teaser rate and purchased homes they really could not afford. Consumers could qualify for these loans because the payment in the beginning was very low. However, when the 3-year, 5-year of 7-year adjustment came due, rates were significantly higher and suddenly payments were going up hundreds of dollars and people could no longer afford the payment in their budget. Therefore, with an adjustable rate mortgage the following disadvantages exist:

- Payment inconsistency after the initial 3-year, 5-year or 7-year period
- Insecurity of not knowing what your payment will be once the adjustment periods begin to take hold

Although I highly discourage them, there are some significant situations where an adjustable rate mortgage can be advantageous. They can be used for financing in one of the following cases:

- You want to minimize the payment for a short period of time until you can get enough to pay for the loan or refinance. This should ONLY be done with the intent of paying off the loan or refinancing before the fixed period (3 or 5 or 7 years) is up. This is the <u>only</u> way this works to your benefit.

- You plan to purchase the home and re-sell it before the fixed period (3 or 5 or 7 years) is up. If you do not plan to keep the house, then you can save with an adjustable rate mortgage.

- Finally, the only other situation where an adjustable rate mortgage can be beneficial is if you are using the mortgage as a temporary loan until you are going to get the fixed loan at the rate you want. In other words, rates are high right now – you expect them to go down, so you get an adjustable rate mortgage for a lower interest rate now – with the anticipation that once the rates go down to a rate you like, you will refinance into a fixed rate loan at the lower rate. Again, you should plan to have the refinance completed before the fixed-rate time period expires.

In my opinion, these are the only instances where getting an adjustable rate mortgage makes sense. Anyone who tries to sell you an adjustable rate mortgage to get you a lower payment so that you can afford a more expensive house that you plan to keep, is selling you a potential disaster. Once the fixed period is up – if you are still in that house with that loan – the adjustments can be extremely high and you can find yourself in a very precarious situation where you can no longer afford the payment.

With respect to amortization, the adjustable rate mortgage is amortized just like a 30-year loan. The fixed time period will be usually be 3 or 5 or 7 years before the interest rate will change. So, for that fixed period, you can plan on the payment being constant at the rate you received. However, once the rate increases, the loan is amortized at the new rate and the payment can adjust significantly. That is all you really need to know. The last mortgage type that I wish to talk about is the balloon mortgage. A balloon mortgage is technically a short term, "non-amortizing" loan. In other words, you will not be paying the loan off completely with the payments at the end of the loan term like you do with a 15-year of 30-year mortgage. Instead, at the end of the term, a portion of the principal will remain and must be paid off in one lump-sum payment – and this is called the "balloon payment". These mortgages typically have lower monthly payments and interest rates. Balloon mortgages are usually fixed-rate mortgages, but the monthly payments that you are making are lower, or, in many cases, may be interest only (interest only loans are a type of balloon mortgage). These loans typically use the 30-year amortization schedule – but the length of the loan may be much shorter and is typically 10, 15 or 20 years. However, even though they are set this way, the actual balloon payment may be due sooner, it all depends how the loan is structured.

For example, if you get a 5-year balloon mortgage, you will have 5-years of standard payments at the interest rate of the loan. If this is not an interest-only balloon, you will be paying down some principal and you will be paying interest.

However, once the 5-year period is up, the balance of the principal due at the time is due – the whole remaining principal. At that point you have the option to possibly refinance with the same lender, obtain another mortgage to pay that principal off or you could sell the house.

So, after reading this, you might ask – why would anyone do this? Again, very similar to the adjustable rate mortgage, the situations where this may be advantageous to you are:

- You want to minimize the payment for a short period of time until you can get enough to pay for the loan or refinance. This should ONLY be done with the intent of paying off the loan or refinancing before the balloon payment is due. This is the only way this works to your benefit.
- You plan to purchase the home and re-sell it before the balloon payment is due (usually an investment situation – and – in that case you might want to do an interest only balloon).
- Finally, the only other situation is if you are using the mortgage as a temporary loan until you are going to get the fixed loan at the rate you want. In other words, rates are high right now – you expect them to go down, so you get a balloon for a lower interest rate now – with the anticipation that once the rates go down to a rate you like, you will refinance into a fixed rate loan at the lower rate. Again you should plan to have the refinance completed before balloon payment is due.

Obviously, the risks or disadvantages to this situation are that you do not do what you need to do before the balloon payment comes due – and you have to come up with all the remaining principal (or all the principal if it is an interest only balloon mortgage) right then and there.

Mortgages or probably the most important consumer financial decision that you will make throughout your life. Hopefully this chapter will give you enough information to choose wisely.

# Chapter 12
# Home Equity Loans / Reverse Mortgages

Now let's analyze two products that deal with property that you own. Since the main points in this book has been understanding consumer financial decisions and effective debt management, these two product address ways to tap into money you already have. Banks and lenders love to discover ways for consumers to tap into that money so they can "spend it and enjoy it today!" (Never mind that you have to pay the money back or whether you really can afford it). Banks and lenders have not only figured out a way for you to tap into money – they get fees and points and all sorts of selling commissions for doing it – so they make money too!

Home equity loans and reverse mortgages can be good products, or extremely bad products if you do not know how or when to use them.

Property is usually a pretty good investment and that the value generally rises. Up until probably 2004 or 2005, this general rule of thumb was pretty good. If you purchase a home for, let's say $200,000 and take a mortgage for $160,000, you start off owing the lender $160,000 and you would have $40,000 in "equity" (equity can be defined as the amount of money you have left if you sold the property today and paid off the loan). Let's assume you have this home for 5 years; you've paid down the mortgage about

$20,000 and the value of the home has stayed constant. Your equity would now be $60,000. (House is still worth $200,000 and you still owe $140,000). But, more realistically, even though you still owe $140,000 it is even more probable that the value of the house has increased, and you actually have even more equity. Let's say the house increased another $25,000. Now if you sold the house you could fetch $225,000 – you still owe $140,000 so your equity value is now $85,000.

So, let's assume you have this $85,000 of money (equity) sitting there invested in a piece of property and you need money to pay bills, fix-up the house, payoff some other debt or to buy a new car or boat or something else. Why not borrow on the "equity" you have in that house?" In other words, there is real value locked up that you cannot get to unless you sell the house. If I can give you a way to tap into that money now – wouldn't that be great? And thus, the home equity loan was born.

Now that you understand it – think about it no more! The home equity loan, in general, is one of the worst products a consumer can get into if they do not have a plan to use the money wisely. If it is just to use the money frivolously, or just to purchase something expensive that you really cannot afford, it can be a terrible financial decision to make.

Generally, you can only take on one of these loans if you have equity in your house. Equity, as we defined above, is the value of your house, after you subtract the amount of principal left to be paid from the loan you have on the house. If you own a home and do not have a loan on it – then you have full equity in the house. If you sold the house today, all the proceeds would go to you free and clear. If you have a loan, the amount of equity you have would be what would be left after you paid off the mortgage loan that was on the house.

So, the real question is – how is the amount of equity you have determined? The key factor is: What is your house worth at any point in time? And therein lies the key piece to this discussion. If the real estate market is doing well today, then technically, your house is worth more (i.e., you could sell it for more) than if you were to sell tomorrow when the real estate market may not be doing so well. So, the way most people find out what their house is worth is they have their house appraised by a real estate appraiser. Another thing they may do is have a real estate agent do a "comp" analysis. A comp analysis is an analysis of properties that have sold in your area that are comparable to your property. So, if your house is 2000 sq. ft., the real estate agent would look for homes in that relative area that were of comparable size and tell you what they sold for. This in turn, would give you a rough estimate of what your property is worth and what it *might* sell for, if you sold it today.

There are a few issues I have with this whole process. First, any piece of property is worth what someone is willing to pay for it at the time you are selling it. While this analysis is close, there is no guarantee that your house could sell for the price that some appraiser says it will sell for. Secondly, if I really want you to take out a home equity loan with me, I might be inclined to inflate the price of what your house is worth, giving you the impression that you could get $20,000 or $30,000 more than what the house would really sell for so that you will think you have more equity to qualify to borrow even more money. Lastly, if you take out one of these equity loans, you are putting yourself deeper into debt by pledging the equity in your home. If, for whatever reason, you suddenly cannot pay this new loan in addition to your mortgage loan, the lender has the right to place a lien on your home and force you to sell to pay off the equity loan. In other words, a home equity loan is risky business.

Finally, remember that, if the real estate market is doing well today, then technically, your house is worth more today than it might be tomorrow. In other words, if real estate is booming today, your house might be worth half a million dollars. You might only have a $150,000 mortgage on it – so that means, at today's prices, you might have $350,000 of equity. Certainly, you can take out a home equity loan for $100,000 and buy a new car – pay off some bills, or just go on a nice vacation, right? Well, guess what? What happens if you take that loan out today and tomorrow (more like 6 months from now), the real estate market tanks and your house is suddenly only worth $200,000. Now you have about $145,000 left on your mortgage and you have about $98,000 left on your home equity loan and suddenly you own more money to the lenders that your house is worth! Even worse, since things in general are not doing well, you are laid off from your job and now you can't really afford to pay your mortgage, let alone, another home equity loan and suddenly you are falling behind in your bills. So, you have a nice new car, went on a nice vacation, but owe more money than your house is worth and you cannot pay for the loans. Not a good place to be!

In other words, the relative equity in your house is a moving target that may go up – but may also go down. If you borrow money against that equity, you are risking taking out money that you really cannot afford to pay back – and worse yet, run the risk of losing your home.

So, does that mean you should never take out a home equity loan? Probably yes, for many people.  It is probably not a good idea to take out one of these loans unless you have a good amount of savings to cover the loan in case you get in trouble.  The irony is that, most people, if they had the savings, would not be trying to take one of the loans to begin with.  You really should not take one of these loans unless you can really afford it in your budget.  If you have done a budget and have enough money left over to pay for one of these loans, then maybe, just maybe, you might be ok to take one.  But if you don't – why would you place yourself in even more debt just to buy something you really can't afford and should not be buying in the first place!

But there can be situations where they can be an effective tool for managing your finances.  Here is a list of where a home equity home can make sense:

- If the interest rates you are paying on some other debts (like credit cards or other loans) is significantly higher than the rate you can get for a home equity loan, taking out a small equity loan to pay off those other loans and bills will be a benefit to you and lower you overall payment.  BUT CAUTION HERE – don't pay off those bills, like credit cards, and then re-spend more money and end up with the equity loan AND the credits card back up to where they were.  This would just be financial suicide and place you in a worse situation that you are now!  If you do this, use restraint and discipline to stay out of the debts you just got rid of.

- Another situation where a home equity loan may make sense is if you are going to use the money to invest in your property to make it more valuable.  In other words, if you have a home that is in need of some major repairs or if you want to significantly upgrade the inside or do fresh landscaping on the outside, it is possible to take out a home equity loan and upgrade your house to the point where the upgrades make the house worth more than the original loan that you took out. This would be investing in your home to make it better and reap the rewards of more than the loan was taken out for. This would make sense if you planned to sell the home soon – or if you wanted to really make the home worth more so that when you do sell it – it would be worth significantly more.

- Finally, the only other situation where taking a home equity loan makes sense is if you have exhausted all avenues for borrowing money to pay for something that where otherwise, you would have to pay a higher interest rate than what you would if you took the home equity loan. This is a somewhat desperate move. For example, if you have some very large bill, like a hospital bill or something else, and the hospital or debt collection service was charging you 12% interest and you could get a home equity loan for only 6% interest, it may make sense at that point to take the loan to pay off the larger debt so that you are paying a smaller percentage of interest on the borrowed amount.

If the loan does not fit into one of these three categories, you should probably not be taking the loan.

Reverse mortgages are another way for older individuals to get money out of their home. (The banks are always looking for way for you to borrow money!) But this actually is one area where I may disagree with some experts, and/or believe that it might be beneficial!

The best definition of a reverse mortgage is from reversemortgages.org and is presented here:

*"A reverse mortgage is a type of loan available to homeowners, 62 years or older, that allows them to convert part of the equity in their home into cash.*

*The product was conceived as a means to help retirees with limited income use the accumulated wealth in their homes to cover basic monthly living expenses and pay for health care. However, there is no restriction how reverse mortgage proceeds are used.*

*The loan is called a reverse mortgage because instead of making monthly payments to a lender, as with a traditional mortgage, **the lender makes payments to the borrower.***
*The borrower is not required to pay back the loan until the home is sold or otherwise vacated. As long as the borrower lives in the home he or she is not required to make any monthly payments towards the loan balance. The borrower must remain current on property taxes, homeowners insurance and condominium fees (if applicable). "*

Once you reach age 62, the government has instituted a program allowing you to take money out of your home (through the equity you have in it) to get PAID by the bank, a monthly allowance or payment – to help with your living expense. Additionally, you can take the loan out for as long as you stay in the home, and, should you exhaust the funds (the available equity) you do not have to pay the bank back or leave the home until you pass away! Of course, once you are gone, if there are no funds left, the bank would own the property and/or your estate handler would have to sell the property and pay the bank back.

Many people don't like this type of loan because they feel they want to leave the house to their heirs. However, if you have no children or no heirs, why would you not do this? You get the benefits of living a better lifestyle in your older years, and when you pass away, you don't have to worry about who your house goes to – the bank will get the house or your heirs will get whatever equity is left.

To be advantageous, the following conditions should exist before you even consider one of these loans:

- You must be at least 62
- You should already have paid off your home (i.e., there is no mortgage or very little mortgage left on the house)
- The real estate market should be pretty good so that the bank will appraise the property at a nice and comfortable price to make it worth taking the reverse mortgage.
- You have talked with your children and or any other heirs and as a family you have decided it is best for you to enjoy the equity for you and your spouse instead of leaving it to someone else when you pass away.

If these conditions exist, and you could really use the income, then by all means consider if it is worthwhile to take such a loan and enjoy your golden years.

However, if, you don't have the discipline to budget yourself and instead spend the equity too quickly or, you would prefer to leave the house to someone when you pass, then you should probably not take such a loan.

Let me give an example to help illustrate this. I knew an individual who, at age 70 became ill. He was living in a wonderful home that was paid off. He decided that he wanted to take a reverse mortgage and get a monthly stipend to help pay some medical costs and to help him with bills. He just wanted to have a little better quality of life – which makes perfect sense. He had no children and he really did not have anyone who he was going to leave his house to.

So, the situation was ideal. Unfortunately, instead of taking a nice monthly allowance of six or seven hundred dollars a month – he took stipends in $10,000 increments and went to a casino and gambled a lot of the money away! After about 2 years, he exhausted all the funds – and was in worse financial shape and health than he was previously. He had to leave the home, since he needed to go to a care facility and the bank wanted him to pay back the loan he had taken (side note here – if his health was well enough, he could have stayed in the home until he passed and just would not have received any more money from the loan for the remainder of his life).

Of course, he could not repay the loan – the bank foreclosed on the home, and he lived a miserable 2 more years in poverty.

The moral of the story is this – reverse mortgages are a great way to help finance your old age – BUT – financial discipline is still in order to ensure you have sufficient funds to finance your golden years until you pass on.

I'll end this chapter with these final thoughts. Taking loans based upon the subjective value of the equity you have in your home is a very risky endeavor. You should only choose to take one of these if you have a thoughtful plan, stay discipline in your budgeting and financial behavior, and/or use the money wisely to improve your overall financial health. If you don't, you run the risk of losing you home and greatly hurting your financial well-being.  Loans based upon home equity are not for the ill-informed or for the novice.  Make sure you know what you are doing – and if you are not sure, talk with someone knowledgeable to make sure you are doing a good thing for yourself and not just appeasing a bad spending habit or making a poor informed financial decision.

# Chapter 13
# Your Credit Score

For many consumers, their first venture into learning about a credit score is probably when they go to apply for a credit card or apply for a car loan or a mortgage. This is when they learn that the financial institutions that lend money rely on the Fair-Isaac Corporation (FICO) rating system to give you a personal credit score number. Based upon their score, it tells them what type of credit risk you are to determine whether they want to lend the money to you or not. So, let's explore exactly what this FICO score is, what it represents and why this is important.

The FICO score tells the prospective lender what type of credit history you have. If you have been extended credit via credit cards, if you have a mortgage, if you have any kind of bills that you pay on payments, all of these are taken into account. The scoring is done using secretive mathematical models but basically uses the following information:

- Your payment history – whether you have always paid on time or if you were late, whether you paid the minimums of more, etc.
- Your current level of indebtedness and you credit utilization. This includes how much debt you have outstanding and how much percentage of the debt is used on revolving credits (i.e., credit cards) vs. the credit limits.

For example, if you have a $10,000 credit limit on your credit card and you have $9,000 charged on that card that would be a 90% utilization on that card.

- Types of credit used – whether they are mortgage loans, equity loans, car loans, credit cards, other installment loans, etc.
- Length of time you have had the credit extended. Here it will say how long you have had the loan. Think about this – if you have had a credit card for 10 years and have always paid on time and never went over your credit limit – this is an excellent indication that you are a worthy borrower. Conversely, if you had only had a car loan for one year and missed two payments or were late a couple times this would be an indication that you are a risky borrower.
- Finally, the last element looked at would be any new or recent credit. Here the thought process would be if you have taken out two or three very recent loans and you are asking to get another loan – you may be getting too much debt too quickly to handle.

These factors are taken into consideration and are fed into the statistical and mathematical models to come up with a score that is between 300 and 850. The lower the number, the more of a credit risk you are and it indicates that you have had issues with your credit payment history in the past and that you are a riskier borrower to lend money to. For example, if your score was 495, this would indicate that you either will be denied the loan or will have to pay a very higher interest rate.

If you had a higher score, let's say 750, this would indicate that you have a very good credit history and that the lender can anticipate that you will pay the loan back promptly. This will win you a very good rating and probable acceptance for the loan and probably a very favorable interest rate for the loan.

For example, let's say you want to buy a new car. When you go to the dealer, you see they have a program to allow you to purchase a car for 0% financing (i.e., interest free). This is an exceptional opportunity and, if you really need a car, would be a wonderful way to be able to purchase the car and pay no interest. However, you should note that the dealership always places a caveat on the program saying you must qualify for the 0% financing. What this generally means is that you probably have to have at least a 700 credit score to qualify. If you don't, you will not qualify and they will probably offer you 3% or 4% or something much higher than 0.

So now that you know what your credit score is and how it is used by lenders to determine whether you get a loan or not or whether you qualify for favorable interest rates on loans, let's look a little more closely at how it works and how you can make your credit score the best it can be.

Remember the factors that I mentioned: payment history, current credit utilization, types of credits or loans, length of time you have had your credit account and most recent credits extended to you (or inquired about).

The most obvious ways to get a higher score is to do the following:

- Always pay on time (nothing is worse for your credit score than to be late with a payment).
- Don't miss any payments. If payments are due every month, pay every month. Do not think that missing a payment and then doubling up later is good. It actually is

really bad for your credit score. Lenders like to see consistency – not unreliability.

- Try not to max out your credit cards to the limit. If a lender sees several credits that are close to 90%, they will be leery of lending you money thinking you may be getting in over your head to handle the additional loan. A good example is that it is better to have 5 credit cards with a $5,000 credit limit on each and only a $1,000 balance on each than to have one credit card with a $5,000 credit limit and a $5,000 balance on it.
- Know your limitations and don't over extend yourself. Lenders can see all the payments you need to make for credit card payments, mortgages, home equity loans, etc. If your income to debt ratio is high (i.e., you need most of your income just to cover the loans), they will not lend to you because they can see that another loan might over-extend you and you will not be able to readily pay back another loan.

So now that you know the key factors, let's look at these a little more closely to see how they affect your score.

As a side note, you should always do a review of your credit score and history. There are several ways to do this. In fact, you can ask the credit rating agencies to give you your latest scores.

I am a big fan of CreditKarma.com. If you sign-up for CreditKarma.com, you will get a window into your score and you can see the factors that affect the score. Below is an example of a report from CreditKarma.com. Note that in this report they are showing two of the largest credit scoring agencies: TransUnion and Equifax. Also note

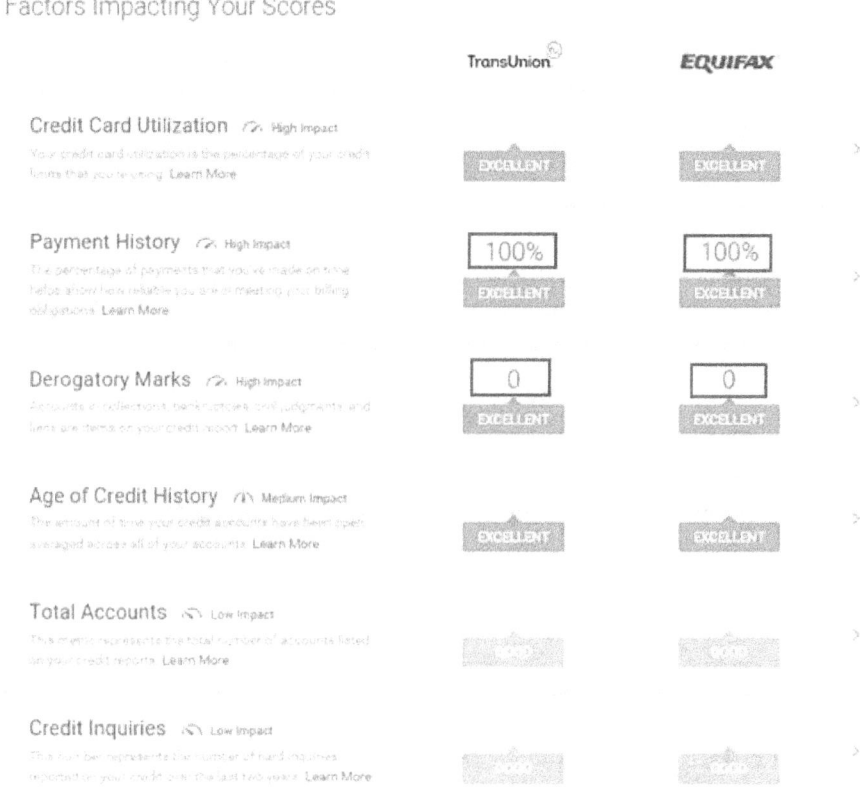

they are showing the "key factors" that affect your score. I have specifically highlighted the two that I believe are the ones that really affect how well your score will be. They are the payment history and the derogatory marks. Your goal is to have those at 100% and 0 respectively. It can, and should be, done.

If, upon reviewing your credit report, you see something that is incorrect, be sure to get it corrected. Your credit report contains all sorts of information about you. In addition to the information presented above (this is a sample report from creditkarma.com) your credit report also has information about where you live,

133

whether you've been arrested or sued, and, foremost, whether you have ever filed for bankruptcy.  This last one is critical because, if you have filed bankruptcy recently, creditors will not want to lend to you because of the risk of you not paying them back.

The credit reporting companies – TransUnion, Equifax, and Experian, all sell your credit information to lenders, credit card companies, insurers, your employer, and any other business that need to evaluate your applications for credit.   Because of this, it is important to review your credit report every so often to ensure the information is timely and accurate.

Below is some extremely helpful information from the following government site about disputing errors in your credit report (**http://www.consumer.ftc.gov/articles/0151-disputing-errors-credit-reports**)

## Correcting Errors

Under the FCRA, both the credit reporting company and the information provider (that is, the person, company, or organization that provides information about you to a credit reporting company) are responsible for correcting inaccurate or incomplete information in your report. To take advantage of all your rights under this law, contact the credit reporting company and the information provider.

### Step One

Tell the credit reporting company, in writing, what information you think is inaccurate. Use our sample dispute letter. Include copies (NOT originals) of documents that support your position. In addition to providing your complete name and address, your letter should clearly identify each item in your report you dispute, state the facts and explain why you dispute the information, and request that it be removed or corrected. You may want to enclose a copy of your report with the items in question circled. Send your letter by certified mail, "return receipt requested," so you can document what the credit reporting company received. Keep copies of your dispute letter and enclosures.

Credit reporting companies must investigate the items in question — usually within 30 days — unless they consider your dispute frivolous. They also must forward all the relevant data you provide about the inaccuracy to the organization that provided the information. After the information provider receives notice of a dispute from the credit reporting company, it must investigate, review the relevant information, and report the results back to the credit reporting company. If the information provider finds the disputed information is inaccurate, it must notify all three nationwide credit reporting companies so they can correct the information in your file.

When the investigation is complete, the credit reporting company must give you the results in writing and a free copy of your report if the dispute results in a change. This free report does not count as your annual free report. If an item is changed or deleted, the credit reporting company cannot put the disputed information back in your file unless the information provider verifies that it is accurate and complete. The credit reporting company also must send you written notice that includes the name, address, and phone number of the information provider.

If you ask, the credit reporting company must send notices of any corrections to anyone who received your report in the past six months. You can have a corrected copy of your report sent to anyone who received a copy during the past two years for employment purposes.

If an investigation doesn't resolve your dispute with the credit reporting company, you can ask that a statement of the dispute be included in your file and in future reports. You also can ask the credit reporting company to provide your statement to anyone who received a copy of your report in the recent past. You can expect to pay a fee for this service.

**Step Two**

Tell the information provider (that is, the person, company, or organization that provides information about you to a credit reporting company), in writing, that you dispute an item in your credit report. Use this sample dispute letter. Include copies (NOT originals) of documents that support your position. If the provider listed an address on your credit report, send your letter to that address. If no address is listed, contact the provider and ask for the correct address to send your letter. If the information provider does not give you an address, you can send your letter to any business address for that provider.

If the provider continues to report the item you disputed to a credit reporting company, it must let the credit reporting company know about your dispute. And if you are correct — that is, if the information you dispute is found to be inaccurate or incomplete — the information provider must tell the credit reporting company to update or delete the item.

# About Your File

Your credit file may not reflect all your credit accounts. Although most national department store and all-purpose bank credit card accounts will be included in your file, not all creditors supply information to credit reporting companies: some local retailers, credit unions, travel, entertainment, and gasoline card companies are among the creditors that don't.

When negative information in your report is accurate, only the passage of time can assure its removal. A credit reporting company can report most accurate negative information for seven years and bankruptcy information for 10 years. Information about an unpaid judgment against you can be reported for seven years or until the statute of limitations runs out, whichever is longer. There is no time limit on reporting: information about criminal convictions; information reported in response to your application for a job that pays more than $75,000 a year; and information reported because you've applied for more than $150,000 worth of credit or life insurance. There is a standard method for calculating the seven-year reporting period. Generally, the period runs from the date that the event took place.

Here are a few more facts that may be beneficial:

- Your credit report can affect whether you get a job. Imagine you are applying to work at a bank and you have filed bankruptcy in the past 3 months. The bank may be very suspicious of you and probably not want you to be a teller!
- Your credit report can affect whether you are approved to rent an apartment. If your credit report shows that you were late paying rent, how confident will the next property owner be with you paying your rent on time to them?
- Your credit report can affect how good of a rate you may get for your car insurance. Insurance companies are huge financial institutions and they make many decisions based

upon statistics and probabilities. If they believe you are a credit risk, your insurance premiums will be higher.

- Your credit report will affect how good an interest rate you will get for a loan, a home mortgage, a car loan, or any other credit. It will also affect whether you get approved for a credit card.

Monitoring your credit report is a very important thing to do. By keeping track of it, making sure it is correct, and doing the right things with your credit, your score will be higher and help you to get better rates for loans, get approved for loans, and help you maintain a healthy financial lifestyle.

# Chapter 14
# Savings Accounts/Money Market Accounts

Up to this point in the book, I have tended to focus on the spending side of the consumer financial world. That is probably because that is the area where most people need a little help or need better information to make informed decisions to help them live a more financially stable life.

But I would like to turn my attention to the other side of the ledger, so to speak. I would like to talk a little bit for the remainder of the book about the saving and investment side of the consumer financial world.

To begin this discussion, remember back in chapter 1 when we discussed the young child who was "saving" five weeks of allowance to buy something that was a little expensive and cost about five weeks' worth of allowance. This is an extreme case of saving all of one's income – but – it at least is showing the tendency to save. Also, remember what happened in that situation. The young person found it very tempting to dip into that savings and suddenly found that their plan to save five weeks did not work as he originally intended.

Most people fall into the same trap as the young child. As much as they would like to save, they just find it terribly difficult or inconvenient or they just stop trying altogether. I've listed here some of the best things you can do to promote a savings account:

- Treat your savings account as a budgeted expense "bill" that you need to pay every month. In other words, to properly save, place a saving item in your budget every month and pay it like you would any other bill. In this case, you are paying yourself.

- If you need to cut into your budget, try to make the savings budgeted item one of the last things you cut

- For an even better situation, consider what was explained in chapter 7 on bank fees. In this case, a small amount was automatically transferred from checking into saving each month. This had a double benefit in that it eliminated the monthly fee for a checking account and it took care of the saving "bill" in the budget automatically.

However, you do it, plan to save something from every paycheck. Where should that money go? In the next chapter we will talk more about investments, 401Ks, stocks, bonds, etc. But for most people, the place where they probably save their money is in a bank or credit union. And the account they usually use to do this is a standard savings account.

Savings accounts, in the old days, used to pay you a modest interest rate for saving your money in the bank. Used to be, you could get 3% or 4% or even more interest on your money. That wasn't bad. Unfortunately, the flip side of that is that mortgage rates were 8% or 9% and borrowing for other loans had even higher rates. So, there is always a good with the bad when it comes to interest rates.

These days, you are lucky if you get 1% annual on your savings account. That is a shame really – because most people are impatient and don't like money sitting in an account where the money is not even keeping pace with the rate of inflation. In this case, an economist would say it is better to spend the money than to save it since you cannot get enough interest to cover the increase in costs. From an economist standpoint – that might make sense. But from a consumer standpoint – it would mean you would be broke and have no savings. Great theory – bad practice!

So even though you only get the ½% or 1%, I still believe it is a good thing to have a saving account. The savings account is nothing special. It is just an account where you save money and calculating the interest you earn is pretty simple. If it is 1% per year, take the money that is in there, multiply it by 1/12 (1% per annual mean 1/12 per month) and that is roughly what your interest should be for the month. You should remember that if you deposited money in the middle of the month, you would only get ½ of the month of interest for that portion of the money that was not in the account. So while I said this was pretty simple, it can get a bit confusing – so let's take a quick example:

In a simple savings account, you have $500 at the beginning of the month. Let's say you have an automatic deposit of $50 on the 15th of the month and you are getting 1% annual interest for the account. The date you get interest just happens to be the 30th of the month (except Feb., where they will give you interest on the 28th). Here would be the calculation for the interest earned this month:

$500 x 15/30 x 1/12 x 1/100 = 0.2083 cents (15 days you had
$500) +
$550 x 15/30 x 1/12 x 1/100 = 0.22917 cents (15 days you had
$550) =
= .4375 cents or 44 cents for this month.

Now, admittedly, 44 cents is not a lot of interest. It almost does
not seem worth it. But, and this is key, if the rate was higher you
would get more interest – and – this is even more key – if you
don't touch this money, the next month you will get interest on the
additional 44 cents. Again, while this may not seem like much,
over time, getting additional interest on your interest is like getting
free money from the bank. And, the more interest you earn, the
more interest on interest you will earn. If the amount in there was
$5,000 instead of 500 and the interest was let's say 5%, the
calculation would look like this for month one:

5000 x 15/30 x 5/12 x 1/100 = $10.4167 +
5050 x 15/30 x 5/12 x 1/100 = $10.5208
= $20.9375 or $20.94 interest.

Even better, on month two you will get an additional 5/12% on the
other $20.94.

The reason I am showing this is because it is important to realize
that whether it be savings, investments, 401K, stocks or bonds, the
way these financial instruments work in your favor is not only the
amount you contribute, but the amount of interest or return you get
because those returns (along with your contributions) also get
additional returns on them – and this is called a "compounding
effect". Nowadays, while the compounding effect in savings

accounts may be minuscule, if rates ever rise, the compounding effect will also rise.

Now let's talk about another account type called money market accounts. Money market accounts are a "hybrid" account in that they look like a savings account, give better interest than a straight savings account, yet they act and feel very similar to a checking account. If that seems confusing – it can be. Just know this – Money Market accounts are really limited checking accounts that are considered savings accounts. Let's dig a little deeper into how these accounts work.

The key to the money market account vs. a regular savings account is that a money market account usually gives you a higher interest rate for your money and it gives you easy access to the money with check writing privileges and even an ATM/Debit card. Unfortunately, these extras come at a cost. Namely, you are limited to usually six or less withdrawals (i.e., cannot write more than six checks or take six withdrawals with an ATM or combination of six) and it usually requires a much higher minimum balance without charging you a fee.

Bank fees are the key for whether this type of account is good for you. In today's low interest rates, it may not make a big difference. But years ago, a money market account paid a significantly higher interest rate than a regular saving account, and you had an easier access to get to your money, if you really needed it.

You should only use a money market account if the following types of situations fit your situation:

- You have a larger balance of cash that you really don't need to access often.
- You want to earn a little bit more interest than a regular savings account.
- You would like to have instant access to the money (like check writing privileges and may want an ATM card) – but you only plan to use this very sparingly.
- You can monitor this account and make sure any fees do not eat up all of the additional interest you will earn.

This is one of the things that many consumers get tripped up on. Banks consider money market accounts as a deposit account – and they always like to have deposit accounts. They want to pay you as little interest as possible, since, they make their money on the difference (known as the spread) in the rate of interest they pay you verses the rate of interest they receive from their loans. So, by placing the high fees on taking out too many withdrawals, or going under the minimum balance, they eat away at the net interest they pay you. For example, if the minimum balance on a money market account is $5,000 and the interest rate is 5%, you can earn a minimum of $250 interest for the year (provided you never go under the $5,000). But if you have more than six withdrawals one month (for a $20 fee) and/or if you go under the $5,000 (for another $20 fee and no interest that month) you can see where the fees can eat away at any addition benefit of additional interest.

You should note that these accounts are federally insured by the FDIC or Credit Union NCUSIF insurance Corps. and they can be effective if you have extra cash you do not need, want to have pretty good access to the money and want to make a better return than a savings account.

As we begin to speak about this other side of the ledger for finances, the savings and investment side, your goal here is to maximize your return on your investment (the interest or dividends that you can earn on your money). That leads us to the next chapter on investments.

*Ken Pyzik*

# Chapter 15
# Introduction to Investments, Retirement savings, 401K, IRAs

I want to touch lightly on a number of investment products to whet your appetite so that hopefully you will do more research into these products and decide for yourself ways to invest your money.

As I mentioned in the preface, just like everyone's spending and financial planning for their expenses is individualized and unique to their particular style, the same can be said for investing their hard earned money.

Essentially, investments are financial products that you are buying. The difference here is that you are buying them for the intention of making more money on the money you are using to buy these things with. To put it more bluntly, no one should be purchasing an investment product unless they intend to make additional money by buying it!

So with investments, you are not buying a loan, or a car, or another consumable product. You are "buying" a financial instrument or product that is going to increase in value so that the money that you invested also increases in value. So let's take a spin at looking at some of the characteristics of these items.

*Stocks*

Most people know what stocks are. But if you don't here is a brief definition. Stocks are an investment in a company. Companies sell "shares" of stock and "shareholders" are people who own shares of stock in the company. Essentially, as a shareholder, you own a portion of the company's assets and you get to share in the company's profits. On the most basic level, you buy shares of stock in a company for a price and hope for the stock price to increase. If you buy 100 shares of company XYZ at $5 a share and the company's share price goes up to $10 a share, you would in essence double your money.

The real value of owning stocks is that your net increase (or your net rate of return on your investment) is usually much better than an interest bearing savings or money market account. Those accounts generally pay you a small amount of interest percentage, and your net return is very small. Stocks on the other hand, can go up significantly and you rate of return on your money is much higher.

As a general comparison, over the real long term (from 1950 to 2014) stocks returned an average of 12.9% per year (according to the calculator at www.moneychimp.com/features/market_cagr.htm). That means, on average, if you invested $1 in 1950 in stocks, it grew to be $1,129.27. By comparison, if you invested that same $1 in a savings account and kept it in there, you would have nowhere near as much. (This is difficult to calculate since rates change all the time and it would depend upon which financial institution you had your savings account with).

But there are some caveats here that you need to know. The general rule of thumb for ALL investments – ***the higher the risk, the higher the potential return.*** This means that stocks come with some inherent risks – the price of the stock could go down and you could lose money. Also, the company for which you have invested money by buying their stock could go bankrupt and you could lose all of your money. This is why people who do not know about stocks stay away from them. Because with stocks, you can lose a lot of money and maybe all your money. With savings accounts, there is little, if any risk, and your money will always grow – much more slowly – but it will grow – and you will not lose any money.

Because of this characteristic of stocks, many people will employ a professional to help them choose which stocks to invest in. This individual, a stock broker, usually makes his/her money by suggesting stocks that they can make a commission on, and/or they charge a fee for their help. For many people this might be a good thing.
However, if you have the time, do your own research and make your own investment decisions when it comes to stocks. If you don't feel comfortable with investing in stocks – then either just stay away from it – or choose someone who you trust to do it for you or with you.

Finally, choose a company that charges the least amount of commission for the buying and selling of stocks. See, when you do purchase and sell stocks, you are charged a commission. Sometimes that commission can be quite significant. However, you can choose a discount brokerage that charges a minimal amount for commissions.

*Bonds*

Another investment is bonds. Bonds come in all sorts of types, characteristics, shapes, sizes, maturity, you name it. Bonds, by definition, are a way for government's, municipalities, utility companies and private companies to issue debt (i.e., borrow money). Different from a bank borrowing money to you, bonds are a way for the government or company to borrow money from people who have money (investors). They are in essence, debt securities issues by governments and corporations.

Bonds can come in many different forms as well. Since a bond is nothing more than a type of loan – many different entities can issue loans. For example – municipalities, government entities, corporations, and public utilities can all issue bonds.

Bonds can be purchased through a stock brokerage. Generally, you buy units (a unit might be in the terms of $25, $50, or $100 increments). The price of the bond at any point in time might be slightly higher or slightly lower than the unit price that that bond was issued as. Additionally, the interest payments for the bond are usually quoted as being paid quarterly, semi-annually or annually. The rate of return for the bond is unusually pre-determined and is paid every period for the life of the bond. Bonds of higher interest rates usually means there is a higher risk that the issuer will not pay back the debt as opposed to bonds with lower interest rates means there is an excellent chance the issuer will pay back the debt.

The table on the next page gives a good comparison of stocks vs. bonds.

## Comparison of Stocks vs. Bonds

| Characteristic | Stock | Bond |
| --- | --- | --- |
| **Financial Product Type** | Equity | Debt |
| **Definition** | A debt where the company issuing it owes the holders money (that was borrowed) and is thus, obliged to repay the principal (amount loaned) plus a predefined interest | Capital (money) raised by a corporation by issuing and distributing shares. These shares give the person an ownership stake in the company. |
| **Owner's Rights** | As an owner of a bond, (called a bond holders) you are essentially a lender; you have lent money to the company or entity that issued the bond | As an owner of stock you own a part of the company; you have an equity stake in the company and share in their profits and share price appreciation. |
| **Who issues** | Bonds are usually issued by several different entities (including government municipalities, credit institutions, companies, etc.) | Stock are usually issued by public corporations. |

| | | |
|---|---|---|
| **Investment characteristics** | More risky; quicker possible growth; higher risk; primarily make money from the stock appreciation; can have some less risky stocks that pay dividends; can lose significant amount of principle. | Conservative; slow growth; lower risk; primarily make money from the interest rate return - some appreciation or depreciation possible. |
| **Level of Knowledge needed to invest** | Moderate level of knowledge. Knowledge of the company, its business, its growth potential; its stability; its profitability; its staying power and influence in the market. | Moderate level of knowledge. The stability and ability for the bond issuer to re-pay the debt; the rating by the bond rating agencies; the level of risk one is willing to take. |

I want to mention one more thing about stocks and bonds before going onto another topic. You should understand how stocks and bonds are "valued".

The price of a stock is determined by people buying and selling the stock on the "Stock Exchange". The stock exchange is a market where stock brokers can buy and sell shares of stock. As an investor, you generally work through a stock brokerage firm who has a "seat" or a place at the exchange, where they can buy and sell shares of stock for you.

Generally speaking, the value of the stock is determined by the value of the company who is issuing the stock. This value is determined by the value of company's assets less liabilities, plus the "net present value of all future earnings". Since the value of future earnings is not an exact number, much of the stock's value is based upon what analysts and buyers perceive the value of those future earnings to be. So if I own shares of stock in a company that everyone thinks has the potential to be a real money maker in the near future, that stock may be worth a lot more than a share of stock in a company that is not perceived to have a lot of future earnings.

Another key factor in determining the stock's value is the expectation of growth in the company's revenue. If investors expect a company to grow very quickly in the near future, the value might be much higher than a company that is expected to shrink or lose revenue in the near future.

So valuing stocks is not an easy thing. It is what the market "thinks" or perceives the value to be of that company and the outlook or future for the company's growth in revenue and earnings.

The value of bonds is a little bit more concrete. Bonds prices are generally determined by how the bond ratings companies rate the future "creditworthiness" of the bond issuer. As an example, if one of the bond rating agencies rates the bond of company XYZ as a "AAA" rating, that would mean that the agency believes very highly that XYZ will honor their repayment of the bond and will have the ability to also pay it back. Generally speaking, bonds with higher ratings (AAA is the highest) will pay a smaller interest rate since there is little or no risk that the investor will not get their money back. Conversely, bonds with lower ratings (B- or C) will have to pay a higher interest rate since there is more risk that they might go bankrupt or may not be able to pay the debt back.

Ken Pyzik

*CDs (certificates of deposit)*

A certificate of deposit (CD) is a type of bank account that allows you to gain a higher rate of interest for your money in exchange for some significant restrictions on the use or withdrawal of the money. You get a certificate which indicated that you have a deposit of money at the financial institution that is for a specified time and for a specified interest rate. For example, if you wanted to buy a $5,000, 1-year CD and the interest rate was 3%, it would mean that you will have that money on deposit at the bank for one year and after that one year you will have $5000 x 1.03 = $5150 (provided it is stated that the interest is paid annually). As long as you leave it in the bank for the entire year (or time length of the CD), you will get all of the interest stated.

The key to CDs is to make sure you never withdraw the money before the time period is up. Generally, if you do this – a significant penalty will be incurred and you will lose the advantage of the higher interest rate return. For example, years ago, a savings account would only get you 1 or 2%. But a 2-year CD might get you 4 or 5% per year. That seems like a great deal. However, if you purchase the CD – remember, it is like placing the money in there and forgetting about it for the next 2-years because if you need the money and attempt to withdraw it, you will incur a significant penalty that will probably eat up all the additional interest you would have earned over a regular savings account.

CDs are a typical investment made by older individuals who want a "simple guaranteed return" for money that they will not be using and to get a better return than just a regular savings account. Another good use for a CD is if you have a lot of money that you need to have in safekeeping and will not need and would like to get a little better return than just a savings account.  For example, Tom and Mary are planning for a wedding and received a $20,000 gift from Mary's grandmother.  But they won't be getting married for another year.  So, they took the money and placed it into a 1-year CD so that they would not be tempted to take the money and at the same time, they would get better interest return on the money after the one year is up.

*Retirement Savings*

Saving for retirement is a very important topic.  Here is something to think about.  Many people don't think that they will live to be 100 years old – and most of them are probably right.  But – if you do live that long and were to retire at 65 (like most people do), it would mean that you still would have 35 years to fund your living expenses – without a real job.

Today, you are able to fund your living expenses because you probably work at a full time job.  If you started working full time at age 18 or 22 (if you went to college), and worked until 65, that would mean that you would have worked 47 or 43 years, respectively, at a full time job.  If you live to 100, that would mean you would be in retirement almost as long as you were working full time (35 years of retirement vs. 47 or 43 years at full time work).

Realistically you will probably live to 80 or 90 and that would mean 15 to 25 years in retirement.  But how are you going to fund those 15 to 25 years if you are not working?  You will get social security from the government because they are taking money from your paycheck to pay for that.  But what if social security is not around once you retire?  Without getting too involved in this topic, every government report I read says that if you are under 50 today

– there will no longer be a social security system like we have today when you get to be 65 at the current rate that baby boomers are retiring (and living longer to drain that fund). Needless to say, funding a retirement account or just saving something for retirement is extremely important. Because if you are not working, how are you going to live?

Realistically, there is no guaranteed way to make money for your retirement. But there are things that you can do that are reasonably safe and that will grow so that you can have some security over your retirement savings.

Here are a few things you can do that would be favorable and give you a good head start on saving for your retirement:

- Open up an IRA (individual retirement account). Depending upon your current income, the money you place in that account may even be tax deductible today.
- Participate in the 401K plan at work – particularly if the company matches your contributions.
- Place a budget item in your everyday budget and call it retirement savings. Even if it is $25 a week – it is better than doing nothing at all.
- Talk with a financial advisor. But a word of caution here – specify to them that you want total control over the money and MINIMAL administrative fees!
- Pay off your house before you turn 62 and then consider a reverse mortgage if you do not plan to leave your home to your heirs

So now that I have discussed the types of things to do – let's explore some of these items in a little more detail.

*401K*

What is a 401K? The first time you heard the term was probably when you were asked at work whether you wanted to participate in the 401K. All your co-workers were probably buzzing about how good or bad a plan it was. And they particularly were talking about the company match. Company match – What is that?

Here is some information that might help you. A 401K plan is a "defined contribution plan" that is offered by a corporation to its employees which allow the employees to set aside part of their pay from their paycheck (as a pre-tax deduction – thus it is tax-deferred) for purposes of saving for their retirement. The nice thing about 401K plans is that many employers will match a certain portion of your contributions as an incentive to get you to participate in the plan. The name "401K' comes from the section in the IRS tax code which describes what they are and how they work.

So, what is the big deal? Well, there is a lot to discuss. First, it is a way for you to save for retirement and do so tax-free until you take the money out when you retire. So, there is an incentive – tax-free money that you can save. Secondly, all earnings in the account are tax-free until you take distributions (withdrawals from the account) once you are retired. Another incentive is that it is an account where your company will match some or all of your contribution – they will give you money – to match your contributions. The amount of the match is different from one company to the next. Another good thing about 401Ks is that is it a way to fund retirement savings in your budget immediately without having to worry about it. The money is deducted from your pay right away (you don't even see it) and it is being placed into an account, that you can manage.

So, with all this "good stuff", why wouldn't someone want to participate in their company's 401K? Well answering this can get a bit complicated. Basically, if there is a company match and you really don't have it in your power to be discipline to save money for retirement – you probably should always participate. But there are some considerations you need to know about that may, just may, prevent you from participating.

First, remember that this money is going for retirement. If you participate at a high level and place a significant amount of your income into this account and then realize you do not have enough money to live on – taking money out of the account will cost you a very dear penalty. You will be charged 10% up front – and – you will get taxed on the money since it was a pre-tax deduction. Moral – make sure this is money you want to earmark for retirement in the first place because once it is in there you don't want to touch it until you retire (well, you can touch it – but it will cost you!)

The second reason some individuals may not participate in a company 401K is because of the investment choices in the 401K. Corporations who offer a 401K generally give it to an investment company to manage. This means you need to sign-up for an account with that investment company in order to participate in the 401K plan. The investment company usually sets up a "basket" of investments – mutual funds, stocks, etc., that you may not know much about. You may be uncomfortable having the investment company selecting your retirement investment options and investing your retirement money into products that you really don't know much about. Although they provide all the information you ask for, you still may not like that you have limited choices of where to invest the money.

But for other than the two reasons I stated above, there really is no reason why someone should not participate in a company sponsored, matching 401K plan. It is probably the best way for anyone to save for their own retirement, it comes to you tax-free until you retire, your company gives you free money as an incentive to participate, and it is an easy painless way to save without even "seeing" the money (since it is deducted right from your paycheck).

The pros clearly outweigh the cons with respect to the 401K. You can change the investments within the plan whenever you want and when you leave the company, your 401K account is "transportable" – meaning it is yours and you can transfer it to the next company's 401K plan or you can place the money into an individual retirement account.

Be careful to make sure if you ever transfer one of these accounts to do so properly. If you do not, you will get charged just like you had a complete distribution. In other words, improper transfer could result in high penalties and income tax levies on the money. To ensure that your transfer is done properly, consult with a knowledgeable person to avoid these penalties and taxes.

*IRAs (Individual retirement accounts)*

Individual retirement accounts, IRAs, are, by definition, any account that you are using to save for retirement. Interestingly, any savings account, brokerage account, stock account, etc., can be earmarked to be an IRA. But what makes an IRA important is the distinction that, once you designate an account to be an IRA, you have placed several restrictions, regulation, tax code laws, etc., in place on that account. The reason for this is because, once an account is designated to be an IRA, you are allowed to contribute (i.e., make deposits) and earn interest or earn appreciation on the money in the account, tax-deferred (i.e., pay no taxes today), until you withdraw the money in retirement (sometime after 59 ½ years old). (NOTE – this is the description of a traditional IRA – we will talk later about another type of IRA called a Roth IRA).

Interestingly, the laws have changed several times regarding IRAs, but these rules are consistent:

- You are allowed to deduct 100% of your contributions (if you are a lower-wage earned) capped at a set amount per year. The amount has changed somewhat, but it is usually between $2,000 and $5,000.
- If you are over 50, you are allowed to contribute even more (called the "catch-up option)
- The money in the account must stay in the account and the earnings as well until you are at least 59 ½. In this way, you can earn interest or appreciation tax-free until you withdraw the money in retirement. The theory here is that when you are working and earning more, you are in a higher tax-bracket and when you retire, you will be in a lower tax-bracket thus saving you money on taxes. It also is an incentive for you to save more to help you self-fund your retirement.
- Once you reach age 70 ½ you must start to take distributions (disbursements/withdrawals) from the account.
- If you start to withdraw from the account once you are 59 1/2, you must at least take annual withdrawals of certain equal amounts or you will be penalized.

There are several other rules associated with IRAs, so you should read up on them before you start one. But the nice thing about

IRAs is that you can save money and earn money now and not get taxed on the money (in fact you probably will get a deduction for your contributions) until you start to take money out once you are in retirement. It is a nice way to save for retirement now without getting taxed.

One specific type of IRA is a Roth IRA. Roth IRAs have taken the concept of IRAs and modified it slightly. Many of the same rules apply except for one major difference – contributions you make today are NOT tax-deductible. The benefit of this is that since the contributions are not tax-deductible, once you retire and start to take distributions, those distributions are tax-free. In other words, if you think you are going to be in a higher tax bracket when you retire, it will be more beneficial to take the tax hit on the contributions today – and get the distributions in the future tax-free.

There are several factors to consider when trying to decide if you want to have a traditional IRA or a Roth IRA. Here are some things to consider. On the next page is a table from the IRS (http://Irs.gov) that gives you some ideas:

| Features | Traditional IRA | Roth IRA |
|---|---|---|
| **Who can contribute?** | You can contribute if you (or your spouse if filing jointly) have taxable compensation but not after you are age 70½ or older. | You can contribute at any age if you (or your spouse if filing jointly) have taxable compensation and your modified adjusted gross income is below certain amounts (see 2014 and 2015 limits). |
| **Are my contributions deductible?** | You can deduct your contributions if you qualify. | Your contributions aren't deductible. |
| **How much can I contribute?** | The most you can contribute to **all** of your traditional and Roth IRAs is the smaller of:<br>• $5,500 (for 2014 and 2015), or $6,500 if you're age 50 or older by the end of the year; or<br>• your taxable compensation for the year. | |
| **What is the deadline to make contributions?** | Your tax return filing deadline (not including extensions). For example, you have until April 15, 2015, to make your 2014 contribution. | |
| **When can I withdraw money?** | You can withdraw money anytime. | |
| **Do I have to take required minimum distributions?** | You must start taking distributions by April 1 following the year in which you turn age 70½ and by December 31 of later years. | Not required if you are the original owner. |
| **Are my withdrawals and distributions taxable?** | Any deductible contributions and earnings you withdraw or that are distributed from your traditional IRA are taxable. Also, if you are under age 59 ½ you may have to pay an additional 10% tax for early withdrawals unless you qualify for an exception. | None if it's a qualified distribution (or a withdrawal that is a qualified distribution). Otherwise, part of the distribution or withdrawal may be taxable. If you are under age 59 ½, you may also have to pay an additional 10% tax for early withdrawals unless you qualify for an exception |

So, there are the several tax rules and implications. But let's break this down a little bit more. For you personally, is it better to have a traditional IRA or a Roth IRA? Here are my opinions – you decide:

- If you believe you will be able to earn a lot of money on interest, dividends, or other value appreciation on the stock or securities you have in the account – you may want to have a Roth IRA. The reason for this is that all distributions from the Roth IRA will be tax-free. On the other hand, all contributions of money you place in the account will not be allowed to be deducted from your taxes when you make those contributions.

- If you want to have a tax-deduction now, and think you will be in a lower tax bracket when you retire, you may want to consider the traditional IRA. You will get a tax deduction now for the contributions of up to a certain amount per year and later, when you retire, you may have to pay tax on the distributions from the account.

Either way you look at it – having and contributing to an IRA is a good thing you should do. It is one of the best ways to help ensure that you will be financially more independent when you retire. Often times, young individuals will forgo an IRA account because they feel that they would rather have money now to spend and enjoy than put money away that they cannot touch (without a penalty) until they are almost 60 years old. But the downside to this thinking is that you lose the growth potential of compounding your money. Consider this:

If you are 21-year-old and invest $10,000 into an IRA and if that IRA can grow at 5% per year on average and you put nothing else in the account – that $10,000 would grow to $89,850 or eight times your original investment if it was in the account for 45 years. Interestingly, if you do the same thing and only add $1000 a year for the next 45 years under the same conditions, after the 45 years you would have $257,535. Now let's get even more dramatic – if you place only $5,000 in an IRA at age 21 and continued to place the same $5,000 for the next 45 years and you could get 6%, you would have $1,196,364! And this would not even include the amount of tax-deductions you would get (assuming it's a traditional IRA) each year on your tax return by being able to take an IRA deduction.

Here is the key – saving for your retirement is one of the best ways to help your financial stability. It also has a dramatic effect on your future lifestyle – particularly if you start EARLY. Start today – put some money away – forget about it for now – and hopefully it will grow, grow, grow!

The last topic I want to cover with respect to IRA has to do with fees. To get a piece of the savings action and value appreciation of your IRA account, several banks, insurance companies, brokerage houses, etc. have decided to charge an annual IRA custodian fee – a fee for taking care of your money while it grows. Don't let them do it! No company should charge you any fee for the privilege of you placing your savings into an account to grow for your retirement. They will contend that they need to "administer" the account by sending you a yearly IRA statement, etc., etc. However, charging an IRA custodian fee is ridiculous. If they try to do this to you – tell then you will transfer the account (roll it over) to another IRA holding company or bank that won't charge you the fee.

I have tried to present a lot of information in only one chapter regarding investment products. However, the best investment advice anyone ever gave me was this – if it sounds too good to be true – it probably is. Choose your investments wisely. Be cautions. Learn to be happy with a slower, steadier rate of return that a "quick buck". This is one area where, generally speaking, and for the most part, the steadier slower more caution investor will more times than not win over the riskier, get rich quick investor.

*Ken Pyzik*

# Chapter 16
# Conclusion – Surviving as a Financial Consumer

As stated in the preface: "Throughout our lifetime, we are bombarded with a myriad of financial decisions that we have to make whether we want to or not. It is not unlikely that you will make a decision regarding your finances at least once a day, every day you are alive. Yet most of us feel ill-prepared to make these decisions."

My goal, from the beginning, was to help make sense out of making financial decisions – personal financial decisions – that will affect you personally for a long period of time. My hope is that after reading this book you will have had at least one of the following happen:

- You will have renewed your commitment to help get your finances under control by taking the information in the book and using it to your personal advantage
- You will have learned some basic mechanics of how all these financial things work;
- You will have been able to at least take one concept in here and apply it to help you make a good, and informed financial decision;

- You will have uncovered something that you did not know before that will help you in the future.

As I have mentioned before, everyone's financial planning, personal financial situation, financial risk tolerance, etc. is about as individualized as each person's personality. In other words, everyone is a little different when it comes to their finances. Some people like to live day by day, while others like to plan out things for months or years in advance. Some don't mind being a little frivolous, while other are very frugal (some might say cheap!). In the end, it really does not matter what your personality or personal finances really are – what matters is that you have the right information to make informed decisions that are right for you – not for the person selling you the financial product. Just because the banker thinks an adjustable rate mortgage is a good way to save a few bucks today – that does not mean it is good for you. Just because the car salesman thinks having all those goodies on the car loan is a good way to get lots of stuff and include it in the loan – does not mean that it going to fit into your budget.

For you to survive as an informed consumer of financial products – I believe it is important for you to understand the simple math and sometimes complex characteristics of those products so that when you decide to get one, it is best for your situation. Be informed and know what dynamics are working in the background that could affect your financial well-being. Nothing could be worse than for you to get yourself into a financial situation that you really can't afford or just feel very uncomfortable about. By knowing how these products work, you can tailor the product to meet with your wants and needs and still fit it into your overall financial plan.

Make informed decisions. From the beginning, your goal should be to stay informed about financial products so that you can make informed decisions. Nothing is worse than to purchase a loan, a car, an investment product (like a stock or bond), and not really know how it works. If you do, you are just letting your financial future and your own well-being be left to chance

Unfortunately, just because you are informed, every decision you make isn't guaranteed to turn out exactly the way you hoped. As it relates to all of these financial decisions, if you lose your job or your main source of income, or if you just fall ill and can't work, or if some unfortunate accident should happen - well, there is just no way you can plan for that and it is difficult to say what the result will be.

However, by making informed decisions I believe it will help you survive the treacherous financial world that can eat you up if you are not careful – just ask anyone who has had tons of credit card debt and no end in sight to paying it off. Someday, somewhere, maybe our schools will teach this information so that young adults can learn at an early age how to really manage their finances.

Thanks for reading – and best of luck in surviving as a financial consumer!

*Ken Pyzik*